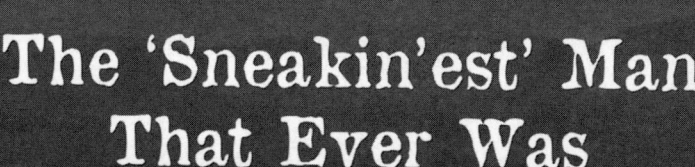

The 'Sneakin'est' Man That Ever Was

Headline Stories of Montana's Early Days

Harmon's Histories Vol. 1

By Jim Harmon

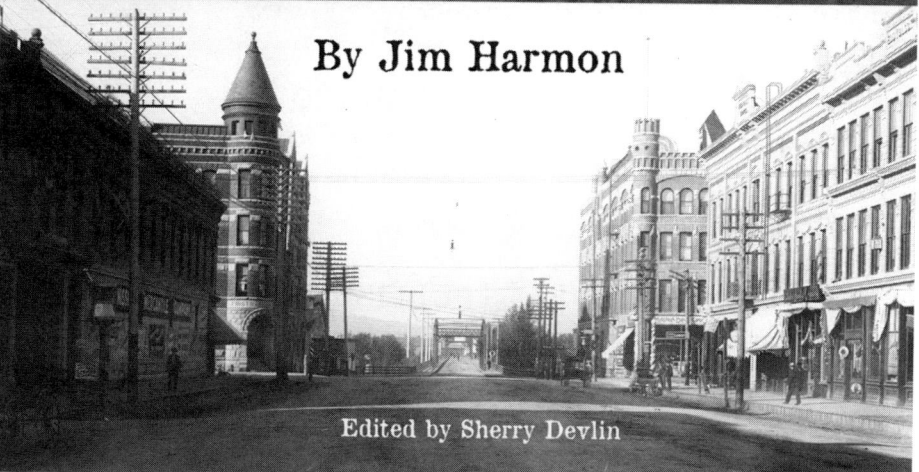

Edited by Sherry Devlin

The 'Sneakin'est' Man That Ever Was

Headline Stories of Montana's Early Days

Harmon's Histories Vol. 1

Jim Harmon

EDITED BY SHERRY DEVLIN

Copyright 2020 by Jim Harmon

ISBN 978-1-938707-57-5

Published in the United States of America

First Edition

ALL RIGHTS RESERVED
No part of this publication may be reproduced, stored in a retrieval system, or transmitted in any form or by any means without the prior written permission of the copyright owner or the publisher.

STONEYDALE PRESS PUBLISHING COMPANY
523 Main Street P.O. Box 188
Stevensville, Montana 59870
Phone: 406-777-2729
Website: www.stoneydale.com

DEDICATION

- To Linda – thank you for your confidence, critiques and enthusiastic support.
- To Molly & Rod – thank you for all you've done in promoting and marketing this work.
- To the online followers – thank you for your encouragement to put these historical accounts in book form.

Author Jim Harmon

ACKNOWLEDGMENTS

• Sherry Devlin, longtime colleague/competitor in the news business, now my editor and friend – thank you for the endless hours spent in making each story just right. You're the best!

• Martin Kidston & *Missoula Current* – thank you for giving me a platform for my writing over the last half decade.

• Keith Belcher, Missoula County Records Center manager – thank you for your considerable assistance in locating historical documents.

• Nathaniel Ball, Archivist and Curator, Elmira College, Elmira, NY – thank you for the Mark Twain collection.

• Deena Mansour, Donna E. McCrea and Mark Fritch, Mansfield Library, University of Montana and Archives and Special Collections – thank you for your assistance and access to the collection.

• Matt Lautzenheiser, Executive Director, and Ted Hughes, Curator of Collections, Historical Museum at Fort Missoula – thank you for your assistance over the years.

TABLE OF CONTENTS

Dedication 3
Acknowledgments 4
Introduction 7
Terminology 8
Preface 9

Characters:
Chapter 1 Coyote Bill – The Sneakin'est Man That Ever Was 11
Chapter 2 Daniel Bandmann – Missoula's Great Tragedian 15
Chapter 3 Dunn Creek Nell – A Most Cantankerous Woman 22
Chapter 4 Swede John, Rastas Reed & the Cedar Beasts 26

Celebrities:
Chapter 5 Mark Twain – International Lecture Tour Reaches
            Montana 31
Chapter 6 Al Jolson – An Instant Hit in Montana 36

Wicked Times:
Chapter 7 Mary Gleim – Queen of the Midway Plaisance 40
Chapter 8 End of the Badlands – The Night the Red Lights
            Went Out 48
Chapter 9 Saloons - "Segar" Smoke, Stale Whiskey & A Fresh
            Croissant 51
Chapter 10 Gunfight on the Higgins Bridge – Train Conductor
            & Dentist Near Death 55
Chapter 11 Murder of a Native Son – Maurice Higgins Fatally Shot 59
Chapter 12 Train No. 58 Hijacked 62
Chapter 13 The Bon Vivant Barber and The Deceitful Dressmaker 66

Progress:
Chapter 14 The Missoula & Cedar-Creek Pioneer – Missoula's
            1st Newspaper 69
Chapter 15 Engine # 452 Arrives – Missoula Becomes a
            Railroad Town 72
Chapter 16 Rails Expand To Bitter Root 78
Chapter 17 Snap & Prince – Missoula's Famous Fire Horses 81
Chapter 18 The Bee Hives – Bargain Stores of the 1800s 85
Chapter 19 A Bridge – A Leopard Skin – A Dead End Street 88

Government:
Chapter 20 House Bill 105 – Missoula is Officially a "Town" 93
Chapter 21 City Council Civility Lost – "Don't Talk to Me That Way,
            You Dirty Little Scrub!" 96

Schools:

Chapter 22 Teachers Institute – Penmanship, Hygiene &
            Boys of Rawhidable Age 99
Chapter 23 Montana's New University – 1st Graduating Class
            of Two 102
Chapter 24 The Janitor & The Football Team – The Beginning
            of The Griz 105
Chapter 25 Cat/Griz – Talking on the Sidelines Cost Griz
            the Game 109

Society:

Chapter 26 The Smart Set – Civility, Culture & Social Order
            in Early Montana 111
Chapter 27 The Bioda Club – Ladies' Kazoo Orchestra 114
Chapter 28 Man In His Proper Place – A Columnist Named
            "Glitter" 117
Chapter 29 Violette Gleamer – Scandalous nom de plume
            Columnist 120

Just For Fun:

Chapter 30 Proper Etiquette – Never Pass Plate More Than Six Times......125
Chapter 31 Helena's Broadwater Hotel – Luxury & Comfort For
            The Elite 128
Chapter 32 Rag Time and Tango – Intolerable, Immoral Dances 132
Chapter 33 Hijinks – The Royal and Universal Order of Mystic Hijis 135
Chapter 34 Hijinks Gone Bad – The Great Turkey Heist of 1893 138
Chapter 35 Lou Lou – Lo Lo – Or, Lolo? 140
Chapter 36 What's In a Name – Cracker City & Baby County 145
Chapter 37 Today's Weather – Flies, Ants & Forecaster Fawcett 148
Chapter 38 Working Girl – The Curious Case of the Crocheted Tidy 153
Chapter 39 Polson's Country Band – Clarinets, Trombones &
            Six Shooters.. 156
Chapter 40 A Fowl Affair – Missoula's Great Poultry Show 159
Chapter 41 Baseball Fever – Potatoes, Rutabagas & Onions
            Fly Through the Air... 162
Chapter 42 Dieting Advice – Walk in Snow, Move to Denver,
            or Commit a Felony 165
Chapter 43 Snake Oil – Restore Manhood, Clean Your Liver,
            & Stave Off Insanity 169
Chapter 44 Bicycle Trip to The Bitter Root – "God Bless The
            Man That Discovered Beer" 173
Chapter 45 The Garden City – Does Missoula Ever Giggle?................. 179
Chapter 46 A Kangaroo in St. Regis – A Cold Breath on My Cheek.......... 182

INTRODUCTION

The quill-drivers of early-day Montana documented it all – the swell-set entertaining lavishly, enjoying Herr Daniel Bandmann's Shakespearean productions at the opera house, while the saloons and houses of Missoula's "Midway Plaisance" gave the city a reputation as one of the worst places in the state for drug-related crime and murder.

Unfortunately we don't know most of these early journalists' names. It's a shame – what great writers they were. Many of the more biting articles were likely penned by the editors of the papers but that will have to remain a mystery. There were no by-lines back then.

If you always thought history teachers and history classes were boring (with notable exceptions like U-M's K. Ross Toole and a few others), you're in good company with this author.

What follows is not a history book – it's a collection of Jim Harmon's short stories based on actual newspaper accounts from the latter 19th century in the *Western Democrat, Northwest Tribune, Missoula Weekly Gazette* and other papers. Also included are some tales passed along from family and friends.

You'll meet characters like Missoula's Coyote Bill and Libby's Dunn Creek Nell. You'll read about visiting celebrities Al Jolson and Mark Twain. You'll likely be both impressed and troubled by accounts of progress and prejudice, while being delighted by quirky accounts of a kangaroo in St. Regis and chicken fanciers in Missoula – and, you'll need to know the lingo of the day.

EARLY JOURNALISTIC TERMINOLGY

- Quill Drivers – Journalists
- Puny Scribbler – A derogatory term for a competing newspaper
- Nom de plume – A pen name
- Swell Set – The well-to-do of society
- Missoula 400 – The well-to-do of society
- Midway Plaisance – The saloons and houses of prostitution along Missoula's Front Street
- Vags – Vagrants
- Hollow Squares – Saloons
- Electric Fluid – Alcohol
- Hotel Ramsey – Jail (insert name of current sheriff)
- Pest House – A reference to a jail or a place housing people with communicable diseases
- Cracker City – Helena
- Baby County – Ravalli County
- Commonwealers – The unemployed who marched on Washington demanding jobs
- Damphools – Damn fools

Preface:

THE MOST BEAUTIFUL, YET WICKEDEST TOWN IN MONTANA

Most Missoulians view their hometown as a progressive center of art, education, culture, beauty and commerce. After all, it is the home of a major university, regional hospitals, shopping venues, tree-lined streets and beautiful homes.

But from its inception to the turn of the 20th century, Missoula was a very different place – one described repeatedly as the roughest and most evil place in the state.

In 1883, a member of Missoula's clergy said he'd seen some of the "lowest dens of infamy" in eastern cities like Philadelphia and New York, but that "the streets of Missoula after nightfall were hell compared to anything he'd seen before."

Murder, train robberies, dynamiting, arson, prostitution and drug use were commonplace. A local newspaper editor admitted that while Missoula was "justly styled the most beautiful of all Montana cities, (it was) yet the wickedest..."

On a single day in August 1891, Missoula's *Gazette* newspaper reported a woman was "nearly kicked to death by a worthless brute who aspired to be her pimp" and "an equally worthless individual who stood by and witnessed the inhuman affair shot himself after being sentenced to sixty days for living in and about the houses of ill-fame."

The sheriff, called to investigate the kicking incident, was "solicited by a woman who was squatting on the door sill of a house" on Front Street. He ordered her to go inside, but instead "she began to revile and abuse the officer, using foul and obscene language," so he arrested her and the "rest of the inmates of the house" and hauled them all before a judge who fined each of them $10.

There were so many cases of arson in a six-month span in 1894 that Judge Frank Woody told a grand jury, "Missoula has the blackest name of any city or town in the state," yet no one had even been arrested, much less convicted. "The situation," he said, "has become a very grave one; human life has been endangered and valuable property destroyed and unless the grand jury takes hold and ferrets out the culprits in these cases," the courts are powerless.

Some of the stories documenting this "wicked period" will be recounted in the pages to follow, but I'll start out with some of memorable characters and celebrities in Missoula, western Montana and northern Idaho.

Chapter 1

COYOTE BILL
THE "SNEAKIN'EST" MAN THAT EVER WAS

Most people simply knew him as "Coyote Bill," the old guy who lived up Missoula's Rattlesnake Valley.

By one account, he was "the sneakin'est man that ever was." He certainly wasn't very neighborly. One man had him arrested on an insanity charge, but it didn't stick. Another had him arrested for blocking a bridge with a rifle. The numerous disputes escalated to the point a couple of men beat him severely, then burned his cabin to the ground.

He was known alternately as Fred Briscoe, K.F. Baskvo, K.E.W. Beeskove, J.F.W. Berkove, W.K.S. Beeskove, K.F.W. Beeskove, William Beeskove, Karolus William F. "Coyote Bill" Beeskove, and Colonel Coyote Bill.

To this day, his name is still in use. A recent forest fire north of Missoula was dubbed the "Beeskove fire" because of its proximity to Beeskove Creek (named after the old codger), which drains into Rattlesnake Creek.

He was a hunter, a trapper and a miner who also claimed to have been a scout for General George Armstrong Custer. He was married five times; in one case, placing an ad in a matrimonial publication before his latest divorce was finalized.

Coyote Bill, seated with rifle, and unidentified companion. Photo from the Anaconda Standard.

He was featured in an 1898 article by M.P. Spencer in *Field and Stream,* titled "Hunting the Big Horn," in which he served as guide to a group of hunters "in the wilds of the Rattlesnake, in Western Montana."

In 1894, Coyote Bill made local headlines for what he didn't do – search for a missing teenager.

Young Bonner Newton, the son of a well-known local carpenter, was in the habit of hunting up the Rattlesnake, where he had befriended Bill. When Newton didn't return to Bill's cabin one night, the old man claimed to have searched for a while, but when he didn't find any sign of the teen, he assumed the young man had returned to town.

Days later, a search party was organized and Newton's body was found. The *Missoulian* gave Coyote Bill Briscoe a journalistic tongue-lashing: "The inconsistency of (his) statements clearly stamps the man as one bereft of ordinary reason. Certainly that is the most charitable construction to place on conduct so unbecoming a human being."

Well, as you might imagine, that didn't go over well with the old hermit.

Coyote Bill's cabin up Rattlesnake Creek, June 23, 1905. Photo from Anaconda Standard.

"Mr. 'Coyote Bill' Briscoe takes exception to the *Missoulian's* reference to his conduct in the matter of the disappearance of his comrade, Bonner Newton, from the Briscoe shack near the Rattlesnake river and has threatened to wipe out the entire staff and all the other beautiful things to be found within the four walls of the *Missoulian* building," the paper reported a few days later.

In 1905, Coyote Bill's irascible nature finally got the best of him. A couple of lumberjacks by the names of Burrig and Smoot were hired by one of Coyote Bill's neighbors to cut firewood on land above the hermit's place.

Bill had always claimed he owned the road and all the property in the area, although many questioned the assertion.

In order to reach the firewood cutting area, the lumberjacks had to break through Bill's locked gate and remove boulders and other obstructions he had placed on the road to discourage trespassers. As the two came down the hill with a load, it would be routine for one of them to drive the wagon while the other sat atop the load with a rifle – keeping an eye out for Bill.

On one such trip, they spotted Coyote Bill, unarmed, and "beat him up pretty bad," according to an account written years later by Forrest Poe, a longtime Missoula resident. During the time Bill was in the hospital, his cabin mysteriously burned down. Of course, Coyote Bill believed it to be the work of the lumberjacks.

After some time had passed and Bill had recovered from the beating, he happened to find one of his assailants on his property again, cutting poles. Bill confronted him, pointing out the property line, marked with blaze marks on tree trunks, but William Burrig ignored him.

Frank Boardman was working with Burrig and witnessed the ensuing argument. Coyote Bill demanded Burrig, "Leave the wood alone." Burrig hissed, "You go to hell!" Then, said Boardman, Coyote Bill shouted, "I will defend my property," and fired two shots at Burrig.

Recounting the event to authorities, Boardman said, "When the first shot was fired, he (Burrig) sank back, and when the second shot was fired he kept staggering back until he fell."

Then Coyote Bill turned to Boardman and said, "You get over the line and stay there and I will not hurt you." Rather than helping the wounded man, Bill then rode to town and turned himself in to the sheriff.

William Burrig was hit in the shoulder and leg. By the time authorities made it up the Rattlesnake Valley to the scene, Burrig bled to death. Coyote Bill was charged with murder, found guilty and sentenced to be hanged. But, on appeal, he was granted a second trial as well as a change of venue to Helena, where he was convicted of manslaughter.

After seven years in prison, Karolus William F. "Coyote Bill" Beeskove relocated to Dixon, where he established an orchard and did some mining. In 1916, he came to Missoula bragging of having filed more than a dozen mining claims near Perma and Dixon, with the prospect of making millions of dollars. In Plains, he told a reporter for the *Sanders County Ledger* he had found a 80-foot-long vein of copper and gold "17 feet square" on Magpie Creek.

As Beeskove bragged, Martha A. Eplin filed a lawsuit in Thompson Falls, disputing the title to some of Coyote Bill's mining claims. The "quiet title" action was designed to have her declared the sole owner of the disputed property and prohibiting any future challenges.

In June 1916, with the jury selected and attorneys for both sides present, the trial was set to begin. But Coyote Bill Beeskove failed to

COYOTE BILL ADJUDGED GUILTY OF MURDER FOR THE KILLING OF WILLIAM BURRIG

Jury in the Case of K. F. W. Beeskove Returns a Verdict of First Degree Murder After Deliberating Less Than Two Hours---Judge Webster Announces That Judgment Will Be Pronounced Monday Afternoon---Prisoner Shows Much Surprise at the Verdict.

Headline from The Daily Missoulian, September 17, 1905.

appear.

One of Beeskove's attorneys, the *Sanders County Ledger* reported, "held the court with an abundance of oratory for several hours, with the expectation or hope that his client might arrive on the next train, but No. 3 rolled in and no Bill. His attorney being unable to hold the court longer by eloquence alone, the judge dismissed the jury and took the case under advisement."

Two days later, Sheriff Hartman set out in search of the man. At Magpie Creek, he found Beeskove lying face down in the water. Subsequent reports said his throat and wrists were cut. Was it murder? Or suicide? No suspect was ever identified; no arrest ever made.

Press accounts varied, but at the time of his death, Beeskove was either 72 or 77 years old.

Chapter 2

MISSOULA'S GREAT TRAGEDIAN
HERR DANIEL BANDMANN

Few got more "ink" in Missoula newspapers in the late 1880s and early 1890s than the man known as the "Great Tragedian."

Daniel Edward Bandmann was a much-acclaimed, world-traveling Shakespearean actor who was born in Bettenhausen, Germany, and emigrated to the U.S. in 1863 as a young 20-something.

A couple of decades later, as part of a U.S. tour, his troupe stopped in Missoula for a four-day gig at a local "opera house." It turned out to be quite memorable. You see, the stage had been built atop an old stable and the aroma on a warm June night in 1884 (how shall we say this?) "flavored" the performances.

Despite that first impression, Bandmann was smitten with Missoula and would soon make it his home.

By this time, the Great Tragedian was well into his 40s, had traveled the world twice and written a book titled, *"An Actor's Tour, or Seventy Thousand Miles with Shakespeare."*

Once settled in Montana in the late 1880s, he produced Shakespearean fare at Missoula opera houses while busying himself purchasing hundreds of acres of ranch land in Hellgate Canyon (known these days as Bandmann Flats), where he raised livestock and planted some of the finest orchards in the state.

Now, saying Bandmann "settled" in Missoula is a bit misleading. He had a home here, but continued to be the "jet-setter" of the 19th century.

Here's an example from a three-month period in 1888. In mid-July, he was in Missoula, but planning a trip to England.

Daniel E. Bandmann, San Francisco Call.

In August, he was receiving an icy reception on a London stage, when his production of *"Jekyll and Hyde"* went seriously wrong.

An overseas dispatch read, "Through an unfortunate mishap in the stage setting and some absurdities of dialogue intended as humor, the performance accounted to little more than burlesque."

Bandmann, photo from Salt Lake Herald, March 31, 1901.

By September of 1888, Bandmann was back on the East Coast, where the *New York Sun* reported: "People about the American Horse Exchange, 50th Street and Broadway, had something to talk about yesterday. Actor Daniel Bandmann headquartered his newly imported stallions and mares there, and at intervals he brought them out to show them to his friends. They are all Percherons, and exceptionally fine ones. ... The entire bunch will be sent to Montana this week to his ranch."

Indeed, the press, from New York to London to Missoula, covered Bandmann's every move, be it on the opera stage, various legal matters, agriculture or ranching. By the 1890s, it was nearly impossible to read a Missoula newspaper without seeing his name. If he announced the cast of characters for a Shakespearean production, it made the paper. If he sold Canadian poplar trees, it was duly reported. If he was having a gopher problem at the ranch, it made news – really.

Clipping from the Western Democrat newspaper in Missoula, May 27, 1894.

The *Western Democrat* newspaper reported: "Anyone who is anxious to kill gophers – go to Daniel E. Bandmann's ranch. Will Cave says it is the best place for gophers he ever saw, he having killed, with M. B. Hendrix, 150 in one day. The next time he went out there, they were just as plentiful."

Not to be outdone, the *Missoulian* newspaper launched wall-to-wall, gopher-to-gopher coverage. "Daniel Bandmann, whose ranch east of this city is infested with gophers and ground squirrels without number," reported the paper, "is in receipt of a small shipment of Ericsson's patent squirrel and gopher bombs, and has arranged for a regular gopher carnival on his ranch for tomorrow morning at 10 o'clock."

In the follow-up report we learned: "The gopher-squirrel exterminating performance at the Bandmann ranch drew out a number of Missoulians. ... The Ericsson bombs were buried and exploded and it is believed that their work was effective. The experiments will be continued."

Even Bandmann's dog made the news: "The rehearsal of the Bandmann company at the opera house, last evening, was greatly enlivened by the frantic maneuverings of Richelieu's prize canine. A reward has been offered for information that will tend to disclose the identity of the misguided individual who had decorated the dog's rear appendage with the theatre dustpan."

Bandmann also operated toll roads and bridges, which rankled more than a few locals, including some Indians who refused to pay and who camped out on Bandmann's property. As the story goes, Bandmann dealt with the Indians by stepping "out of his door in a terrifying costume, reciting theatrical lines at the top of his voice (while) switching languages from German to English to French."

He would then go back inside and watch "as the Indians gathered round in consultation, then systematically packed up and moved on, never to use his yard as a camping spot again."

Humorous references to Bandmann's toll roads and bridges were rare – more commonly his enterprises led to lawsuits and assaults, while his women-troubles threatened to do him in.

Herr Daniel E. Bandmann may have been a much-acclaimed, world-traveling Shakespearean actor, but he also could be a cranky and confrontational ass.

A *Kansas City Journal* article May 4, 1898, claimed nearly every interaction Bandmann had resulted in either a lawsuit or a fight, pointing to an incident in which Bandmann had failed to follow through with a business deal he'd made with his dentist, Dr. Oettinger. The dentist lured Bandmann to his office "under pretext of examining Bandmann's able-bodied feed-choppers," snatched out the store-bought teeth and pocketed them.

The outraged Bandmann attacked Dr. Oettinger, and for a short time had the advantage until the dentist grabbed one of his "implements of torture, which was fortunately within reach, with which he proceeded to jab Bandmann in the nether portion of his anatomy where the bosom of the pants are supposed to be located." Neighboring businessmen, hearing the melee, broke up the fight. Oettinger, reported the newspaper, "still holds the teeth, however, and Bandmann is hunting for a lawyer who will replevin them, though in the meantime he is feeding his face with a spoon."

Headline from a newspaper story about Bandmann's "teeth" problems.

Another time, when he got in an argument with a ranch employee over wages, the *Missoulian* reported Bandmann, "evidently emulating the practices and actions of Herr James Corbett, did strike, knock down and hit with his fists one James Guthans. At least so says a complaint sworn to in Judge Donnelly's court, charging Daniel E. with assault and battery."

Bandmann denied the charge and characterized his accuser, Guthans, as "a tramp, an anarchist, dynamiter and numerous other unpleasant things, and accused him, together with his attorney, Mr. Prince, of having entered into a conspiracy to extort money from him and the taxpayers of Missoula County."

In another case, Bandmann had a falling out with the keeper of his toll bridge and charged him with embezzlement, only to be arrested himself "on a charge of obstructing a public highway."

A few days later, Bandmann sent a letter to the editor of the *Western Democrat* newspaper claiming his "spiteful neighbors" were out to get him by circulating a "petition that my bridges were rotten, that if they were not rotten the toll was too high."

In yet another argument over the toll bridge, a neighboring farmer named Cook "ferociously" beat Bandmann with a scoop shovel. The actor claimed it was attempted murder. Cook claimed it was self-defense. The trial featured "ludicrous and contradictory" evidence.

One particular press account summed it up in a single, hundred-proof sentence: "The prosecuting witness and his supporters claim that the wounds inflicted upon the person of Mr. Bandmann are entirely due to the assault alleged to have been made by Mr. Cook, while the testimony for the defense is to the effect that the complainant tore and bruised himself by falling over ditches and jumping through barbed wire fences in his attempts to escape from the defendant, who was exceedingly angry at the treatment he had received at the hands of Mr.

Bandmann's toll-gate keeper." (That sentence gives me flashbacks to diagramming assignments in high school English class).

In the end, the best the jury could do was to halfway convict Mr. Cook by fining him $5 and costs.

Yet Bandmann's real downfall was his weakness for the ladies. In the mid-1860s, he married Anne Hershel of Davenport, Iowa. The marriage lasted only a short time; they had no children.

A few years later, at age 28, he traveled to London, where he married 23-year-old Millicent Palmer; they had two children.

In 1879, while on an Asia-Pacific tour with his actress-wife Millicent, Bandmann had an open affair with the beautiful ingenue Louise (Louisa) Beaudet, whom he had elevated to stardom after being smitten with "the girl's wonderful intelligence and personal attractions … (graceful) figure … (and) eyes sparkling with fire."

That's when things started to unravel. Millicent returned to London. The actor started parading Louisa Beaudet about, introducing her as "Mrs. Bandmann," only to abruptly dump Beaudet (who then sued him for breach of contract, forcing him to pay her off to avoid a messy court trial) so he could marry Mary Therese Kelly in 1892. Did I mention Mary was with child?

Of course, all this time Daniel was still married to Millicent, so he engaged a couple of lawyers to file divorce papers, inexplicably in Park County, where he was not a resident (perhaps to try to avoid publicity).

Louisa Beaudet, Albuquerque Morning Journal, April 18, 1916.

The lawyers, one of whom happened to be Iullus Greenleaf Denny, better known as I.G. and who would soon become Missoula County attorney, claimed Millicent had simply disappeared, abandoning poor Bandmann. Despite their best efforts, they said, her location could not "with due diligence be ascertained." So the court granted the divorce.

The trouble was, the lawyers didn't try very hard to find Millicent. She was sitting in the Bandmann family home in London, a home purchased years earlier by the couple, a home Daniel obviously knew about – but perhaps forgot to mention to his attorneys?

> **BANDMANN--BEAUDET**
>
> **The Tragedian Sues His Erstwhile Leading Lady.**

Headline from the Missoula Weekly Gazette, September 30, 1891.

Upon learning of the goings-on in Montana, Millicent fired back, saying (in effect) if there was any abandoning going on, it was on the part of her two-timing husband. She directed her London barrister to sue Bandmann for divorce.

She demanded alimony, child support and property, citing years of cruel and violent treatment at the hands of Herr Bandmann. Millicent also claimed that her husband had numerous affairs over the years with "various women other than Mary Kelly."

Oh, by the way, Millicent pointed out that Bandmann certainly knew where she was since he'd been sending support money ($2,000 a year) for nearly a decade before cutting her off. Her lawyer asserted Bandmann was worth over $20,000 and his client wanted her fair share. He told the court the real "Mrs. Bandmann" had worked side-by-side with the famous actor, helping to earn that money, something to which Louisa Beaudet could attest. Further, they asked the court to freeze his assets.

> **HERR BANDMAN DIES SUDDENLY**
>
> **WORLD RENOWNED ACTOR DROPS DEAD AT HIS RANCH NEAR MISSOULA.**

Headline upon Bandmann's death from the Fergus County News, Lewistown, Montana, November 28, 1905.

Bandmann countersued, reasserting his claim that Millie was the deserter; abandoning him "without cause" and "against his will." To make a long story short, Bandmann finally agreed to pay support and the two were divorced. But when it came to actual payment of the agreed-upon child support, Bandmann was disingenuous. He failed to pay on time, or at all, forcing Millicent to repeatedly return to court.

Over time, though, it became clear Bandmann actually was in financial trouble. Millie stopped pursuing him in court, and the record showed no further action.

A decade later, on November 23, 1905, (only months after the birth of his final child, Daniel Jr.), Daniel Edward Bandmann, one of the greatest Shakespearean actors of the day, complained of severe indigestion and dropped dead of a heart attack at his ranch. He was 66.

Daniel Bandmann (L) with daughters Eva and Susan next to him. Bandmann's wife, Mary Therese, is sitting next to the house with daughter Hebe standing in front of her. The other family are unidentified. Circa 1902. Photo courtesy Mansfield Library, Achives and Special Collections, University of Montana – Missoula.

Chapter 3

DUNN CREEK NELL
A MOST CANTANKEROUS & CONTRARY WOMAN:

She went by the name Docia. But most folks knew her solely by her nickname, Dunn Creek Nell, a reference to her family's property along Dunn Creek where it flows into the Kootenai River northeast of Libby.

From the early 1900s until her death in 1967, she was a local legend. Some said she terrified a young neighbor girl, telling her she'd had 17 husbands and burned them all in the cookstove. There were all sorts of stories like that. But the question was: How much was talk and how much was truth?

Dr. Pat Neils, whose husband's grandfather founded the local lumber company, spent considerable time researching the mysterious woman. Neils wrote and lectured extensively about Docia, describing her as "the wildest, most cantankerous and contrary woman who ever passed through these parts."

She was born Sara Theodocia (Docia) Yeary in 1879 in Anita, Texas. Mary Frederickson, in the book *Pages From The Past,* published by the Libby Writers Group, described Docia as having a "happy early childhood ... riding across the Texas prairie on her white horse." She attended a girls' finishing school until her family went broke. Libby's newspaper, the *Western News,* reported "she came to the Libby area with her mother and stepfather when she was still in her teens."

Frederickson, however, found that as a teen Docia was sent to stay with an "Aunt Bess" who ran a bordello in Butte. Later, she "hopped a train" to Wallace, Idaho, where she worked in a bordello and later in a dance hall. It wasn't until 1900, at age 21, that she headed to Libby where her parents had begun to establish a homestead on Dunn Creek.

Despite her education, Docia showed no sign of ever having attended a finishing school. She was described variously as rude, loud, wild and/or cantankerous. She seemed to have an insatiable desire to be married. The number of husbands is uncertain, but Mary Frederickson listed six of them: Turner, Tigner, Daniels, Ali, Sultas and Guffee. Hassan Ali, known in Libby as "The Turk," was a colorful character who wore "a big white turban and large signet ring."

As she moved on from one husband to another, rumors circulated that she killed some or all of them. None of the rumors was ever substantiated. It's much more likely the husbands (whatever their number) just tired of being around the woman and left of their own accord.

Some folks believed Docia just loved to tell a good story and was overly theatrical. That was reflected in a comment on the *Western News'* Facebook page by a woman who said, Docia "was delightful and could tell stories like no other. I enjoyed knowing her."

One undisputed fact was her connection with the J. Neils Lumber Company from the late 1930s into the 1940s. Dr. Pat Neils, writing in *Montana Magazine* in 1981, said George Neils was "one of the few people (Nell) trusted and respected." George won her trust by negotiating a right-of-way through her property to their timber stands in exchange for the company installing a water system to her cabin.

> **Logging Camps**
>
> J. Neils Lumber Co. continued to operate logging camps into the 1950s. The company completed its cutting south of Libby in 1936 and transferred much of its energy to a new sale near Leonia. A large camp there, built under the supervision of Frank Pival, accommodated 100 men (*Timberman*, December 1936:91). In 1938, crews also set up another camp along the railroad tracks at Dunn Creek, near Warland. This camp was there until c. 1950 and then was moved to the Rexford area where it operated until c. 1958 (Neils 1976:23-24).

Montana Memory Project – Historic Overview of The Kootenai National Forest Southern Region, Volume I, p.259.

The Neils Company set up its camp along the rail line where Dunn Creek runs into the Kootenai River. Pat Neils says George hired Nell "as a camp guard," watching over buildings and equipment when the company wasn't actively logging. They paid her $30 a month.

My grandfather, John Harmon, worked at various times for the J. Neils Lumber Company, both before and after a stint as Libby's police chief. He liked to tell the family one particular story about a run-in with the mercurial Dunn Creek Nell – a story retold years later by my dad. "George (Neils) had gone up and talked with Dunn Creek Nell and made arrangements that they were going to start logging up there."

Clem West, a company surveyor, according to my dad, "quite often asked (John) to go along and pack stakes for him and (help) run some survey lines." The lumber company had arranged for a boat to be left for the two men to get across the river to the logging site. "When they got down to the boat, they (saw the company) had a couple of boxes of dynamite and a box of caps thrown into the boat for them to take across and leave over there."

Lee said, "Dad and Clem started across the river that morning rowing the boat (when) something went 'ping,' and bounced off the water, and 'ping' again. Clem says 'Darned, I think that crazy old woman is shootin' at us.' and dad said, 'Let's get out of here!'" The two rowed back across the Kootenai River and headed into town to report to George Neils that they "didn't get the work done because they couldn't get over there." My grandfather was "darned happy when he got home that night he didn't have a hole in his hat!"

> "I had dealings with one or two such women who would just as soon shoot you as not. She lived at the mouth of Dunn Creek just off the Kotoenai River." – **Leon Lake**, writing in *Early Days In The Forest Service, Vol. 3.*

Leon L. Lake, who retired from the Forest Service in 1951, also knew firsthand about Nell and her tendency to go for her gun. He was sent out to deal with Nell after she had fenced off the access road to the logging operation. When he knocked on Nell's cabin door, "She opened it, and immediately dashed for her .30-06 rifle, threw a shell into the chamber, and laid it across the table. I asked her why the rifle, and she said that she was always prepared for action. I opened up my coat and made the statement that I always went armed also."

Writing for a U.S. Forest Service publication, Lake recalled, "She cussed and raved about the J. Neils Lumber Company and what thieves they were, along with the forest officers who all robbed poor widow women." Lake said she threatened to "shoot every last man (who came up there) and roll them over the bank." Given her threats, Lake changed tactics, telling her they wouldn't be able to help her should a forest fire break out on her property – they'd just have to let it burn until it reached the fence. "She thought a minute and said, 'Let's tear the G.D. fence out.'"

Around 1930 or so my dad, Lee, had his first encounter with Nell when he was working as a teenage weekend usher at Libby's Dome Theater. "During all the old Westerns with Tom Mix, she'd stand up and yell, 'Come on Tom! Get 'em, Tom!' I'd have to go down and try to quiet her down. The only way I could quiet her was by saying, 'Nell, if you don't shut up, I'm going to throw you out that door!' She'd give me a look, and she'd settle down for five minutes and then we'd be back at it again!"

Later, when Lee worked for the Plummer family, who were neighbors and owned the local mercantile, Nell would come to the store for provisions. "She'd come in with a rugged-looking old shopping bag, all rolled up," said my dad. "One day she gave me her grocery order, saying, 'I'll be back. I gotta go over to the ladies ready-to-wear.' She was gone for quite a while, so I got the order put up and I thought, well, I could put it in her bag for her. I opened it up and saw a rifle in the bottom of that bag (presumably her trademark Winchester model 1895 repeating rifle). Just then, she came back and she lit into me, 'Don't you ever open my shopping bag again or I'll take care a you!'"

By the 1960s, Docia and her husband, Carl "Slim" Hovis, both in poor health, are said to have moved to a cabin closer to town. Docia was in her 80s and virtually blind. Slim was reportedly serving her meals, which she'd eat with her hands. Pat

Lee Harmon with parents, John and Pauline Harmon, circa 1942.

Neils says when Hovis died, Docia was taken to a convalescent home. "She hated it there and gave the nurses a very hard time." Later, she was transferred to Warm Springs for mental evaluation and care. She died there on February 27, 1967.

Paul Sievers, a retired photographer at the *Western News*, tells me he discovered – after some digging through courthouse records – that Nell was buried next to a tree in an unmarked grave at the Libby cemetery. That's a shame. She was a character, and characters are a big part of Montana history. Someone described as "the wildest, most cantankerous and contrary woman who ever passed though these parts" should have a more fitting marker, reflecting her place in Montana's past.

Chapter 4

SWEDE JOHN, RASTUS REED
AND THE CEDAR BEASTS

Jack Puckett is a great storyteller and a good friend. He was born in Burgettstown, Pennsylvania, on April 18, 1927, entered the U. S. Navy in 1945 (serving briefly on a destroyer in the South Pacific) and in 1950 graduated from Penn State with a degree in forestry.

Jack Puckett

For the next 32 years, Jack worked for the U. S. Forest Service in northern Idaho and Montana. Along the way, he encountered (or heard about) a variety of backwoods characters, among them "The Cedar Beasts," "Swede John," and "Rastus Reed." With Jack's permission, I'm sharing some of those stories. One of my favorites is the tale of Rastus Reed.

Rastus was an older fellow, probably in his fifties when he came to work for the U.S.F.S. "In those days, when you hired a guy for longer than six months, you had to fill out an extra form that wanted more information on the poor soul," Jack recalls. One question asked if the applicant had ever been in jail. "Well, Rastus was a little reluctant to say," but he finally admitted there was that one time long ago, "back east in Kentucky or someplace." Jack figured it no big deal and gave the fellow a break.

Rastus was hard to miss in a crowd. He wore an old mackinaw coat, a red hat, and was always accompanied by his dog, Spot, who could hardly get around. Jack figured the dog was probably about as old as Rastus. When Rastus "was doing something physical, he'd take the coat off, lay it down and the dog would lie on the coat. That's the way it went."

Jack's crews always worked hard, he says, "but they also liked to drink" – especially Rastus. You could always hear him approaching, given his ever-present supply of beer. He kept it in a big pouch in the back of that mackinaw coat. Beer, back in those days, came in glass bottles "and you could hear the bottles clinking as he came walking down the street."

Now and then Rastus wouldn't show up for work. That would generally be on a Monday morning. "I went over one day. His cabin door was shut, so I knocked on the door and pretty soon here comes Rastus and I says, 'You coming to work today, Ras?' 'Oh,' he says, 'No, I don't feel very good; I think I had a bad can of beans.' Of course, he'd been drinking all weekend – but the beans were what got him!"

Jack recalls, "We were on a fire one time. I came around the fire line and old Rastus was digging out a stump and he's working hard and sweating. And so I said, 'Hey Rastus, take a break here.' So he sat down. "I thought I'd 'job him' a little bit. I said, 'Boy, wouldn't a cold beer go good now?' He said, 'Oh yeah, yeah.' I asked, 'Don't you wish you had some?' And he says, 'What makes you think I don't?'" He showed Jack the back of his coat – it was full of beer! "He was a nice guy who just had a little drinking problem at times."

When Jack worked on the Priest Lake District of the Kaniksu National Forest, he encountered a number of fellows who contracted with the Forest Service. They'd set up cabins and work all winter making cedar poles and posts in the backcountry.

"They didn't seem to have families. They were lone individuals. We had a picture on the wall in the ranger station of the 'cedar savages' or 'cedar beasts,'" as they were known.

"They'd snowshoe out every once in a while to get groceries, then snowshoe back in and go at their cedar work," recalled Jack. "I don't think they worked every day, but they'd stay in their cabins. They had plenty of wood from scraps to keep warm."

One time, the ranger on the district became concerned about one of the "cedar beasts." This particular fellow hadn't come out of the backcountry for some time, so the ranger and the "alternate" (the assistant ranger) decided to snowshoe in and see what was going on.

"They got to the cabin and it was all quiet around there. They opened the door and the old cedar maker is there, sitting at the table, slumped over, dead!" He'd apparently been there for some time.

"So the assistant says to the ranger, 'What are we going to do now?' "The ranger," as Jack tells the story, thought for a moment, then "pulled out a chair, sat down at the table" and calmly replied, "I don't know about you. I'm going to eat my lunch!"

Much of the Powell Ranger District was inaccessible by road. So when there was a forest fire, they depended on packers and their teams to shuttle in supplies and food.

"The packers always checked their cargo the night before, except for the fresh stuff, so they'd be all ready to load," said Jack. "The next morning they'd saddle up their string, then go to breakfast before loading the packs."

Jack watched as one of the packers checked his cargo. He'd met the man before and knew he was experienced and reliable. "He finished up and went down to the bunk house, and then here comes one of the guys from the station.

"He goes over and he looks 'em over and he hefts the load, and pretty soon here comes another guy. He checked him out, lifted the load. I got a kick out of that because they were checking to see whether he had done a good job.

"The next morning, the packer readied his string of nine mules and loaded up, with the Forest Service guys all standing around watching. He picked up his lead rope, swung up on his saddle horse and took off down across the flat, and never looked back!"

Jack said, "When you didn't have to look back to see if a pack is going to slip, you had it made. And away he went."

Another time, the forest supervisor was showing someone from the Washington office around. As they watched a packer working, "that guy from the Washington office, he says, 'Doesn't he need help?' The supervisor says, 'No, he doesn't need any help. Just watch.'

"Sure enough, he loads up all those mules, swings on his horse, takes off with two strings of mules and never looked back. And it was kind of remarkable because that's a lot of mules to have – 18 mules behind you – when you're going out on the string."

Another character, a packer who ended every sentence with "by God," had a love for bagpipes, but had a tin ear.

"He couldn't probably carry a tune to save his soul," said Jack, "but he would practice on this chanter – it's like a little part of the bagpipe, the part where they finger the holes and it makes a noise.

"He would have a record player and he would turn it up as loud as he could. Then he'd go out in the corral with the mules and he would be practicing on his chanter." The cacophony could be heard for miles.

The bagpipe lover didn't love everything; he had a serious dislike for helicopters. "He could see that the helicopter was about to replace the pack string," said Jack, "and he didn't want that to happen."

One day, Jack went up to Elk Summit where there was a little warehouse, only to find a "big gob of aluminum tacked up on the side of the building and a little sign under it that said, 'Helicopter presumably killed by 44 magnum'" – most likely left by the bagpipe packer.

Another character was Mel Kolander. He was one of the so-called "cedar beasts" up on the Kaniksu. As the moniker implied, none of these guys were known for their cleanliness or social graces.

Old Mel "lived in a little shack in the woods," said Jack, "and my job, at times, would be to go up and scale the logs and measure the poles and count the posts. The pole company was charged accordingly and then they apparently paid these guys whatever it was that they could get them to work for.

"One of the first times I went up to talk to him and scale up his stuff, he had an old Hudson car and he was out there trying to crank on it and get it going. He says, 'Get in there and pull out that throttle when I turn the crank.'"

Once they got the car running, Mel said, "What you need now is a cold drink." Jack figured it was going to be a beer, but instead Mel said, "I have the best spring in the county. I'm going to make you a glass of 'Koolaid.'

"He fished around in the dish pan and he found this old greasy cup and put some 'Koolaid' in there and some of this great spring water and he handed it to me and it almost slipped out of my hand! Now do you make the guy mad by refusing to drink it? Not I. I swilled it down gravely and decided maybe I didn't need to count too many poles that day."

Another time, Jack went up to take mail to Mel on a wintry day. "I got to his shack. The stove was going full bore and he was washing his shirt. Now he had his sleeves rolled up and you could see how far he'd had his arm in the water. There was a watermark on his arm.

"As he was washing these clothes, he had hamburger cooking on top of a stove – he had it laying there, no pan or anything, with the juice running off and down the side of the stove. I was afraid he was gonna ask me to stay for lunch. I decided maybe I'd just leave his mail and go."

Another character who lived just up the road from the ranger station was friendly enough. He'd wave at passersby. Jack remembered he had a little bit of land, "a couple cows, maybe a sheep or two, a couple of dogs and maybe a half a dozen cats."

Jack didn't know the man's name, but an outfitter at Clarkia told him the fellow was known as Swede John, and he was a bulldozer operator.

The outfitter told Jack, "You know, I wanted Swede to come help me here a few days ago. And so I went over to get him in the morning and old Swede was just eatin' his breakfast and so he invited me to sit down and eat with him."

The outfitter declined – a good choice, as it turned out. He told Jack, "Swede finished off this hotcake and then held his plate down and the dog licked it off. He put the plate back on the shelf and he was ready to go to work!"

Chapter 5

MARK TWAIN TAKES A WRONG TURN ON WAY TO FT. MISSOULA

Aboard the coach making its way from the train station to the Florence Hotel in Missoula, he observed a man riding a bicycle and leading a horse. He suggested that his companion snap a photo of the scene, offering up the caption: "There's Missoula up to date."

It was the afternoon of August 5, 1895. The man was Samuel Langhorne Clemens (aka Mark Twain). The photo enthusiast and companion

Twain: "There's Missoula up to date." Photo courtesy Mark Twain Archive, Elmira College, Elmira, NY.

Mark Twain and Senator Wilbur F. Sanders, Missoula, Montana, August 5, 1895. Photo courtesy Mark Twain Archive, Elmira College, Elmira, NY.

was his business agent Major James B. Pond.

Clemens, penniless and in ill health, was on the first leg of a two-year international lecture tour to raise money and repay his creditors. Accompanying Clemens were his wife, daughter Clara, and Major Pond and his wife.

The Missoula stop was one of five in Montana, and one of 23 performances in 22 cities from Cleveland to

Vancouver, British Columbia. Pond kept a journal of the trip across the continent, intending eventually to write a book. Throughout the journal, he was consistent in referring to Clemens as "Twain."

The first Montana stop was in Great Falls on Wednesday, July 31, 1895. Pond observed, "The Falls could supply power enough for all the machinery west of Chicago, with some to spare." As he and Twain walked about town, Pond took a number of photos, including some in a local Norwegian shanty neighborhood where children were playing with kittens. He later wrote, "Few know Mark's great love for cats, as well as for every living creature."

Pond described Twain's performance the next night in Butte as "off," saying Twain "was not at his best, which has almost broken his heart. He couldn't get over it all day." Pond himself was out of sorts too. While acknowledging, "The Gibson Brothers have done much to make our visit delightful," he added, "Of course, being proprietors of the hotel, they lose nothing, for I find they charge us five dollars a day each, and the extortions from porters, baggage men and bellboys surpass anything I know of. The smallest money is two bits (25 cents) here – absurd!"

John Maguire has secured Mark Twain to lecture in Butte and Anaconda at an early date. The famous humorist is about to take a trip around the world on a lecturing tour and will sail from San Francisco early in August for Australia, India, South Africa and thence to London.

Twain tour announced in the Anaconda Standard, June 21, 1895.

Twain's second performance in Butte, the following day, August 2, 1895, was far better. Pond wrote, "I found myself listening … enjoying every word. It actually seemed as if I had never known him to be quite so good. He was great. The house was full and very responsive."

Following the performance the pair boarded a trolley to the train station, but within a few blocks it broke down. So they flagged down a passing grocery wagon, "but the mean owner refused to take us a quarter of a mile to the depot for less than ten dollars. I (Pond) told him to go to ----. I saw another grocery wagon nearby and told its owner I would pay any price to reach that train.

"Mark and I mounted the seat with him. He laid the lash on his pair of broncos, and I think quicker time was never made to that depot. We reached the train just as the conductor shouted 'All aboard!' The driver charged me a dollar, but I handed him two."

From Anaconda, it was on to Helena, where Pond lamented "people did not care for lectures. They all liked Mark and enjoyed meeting him, but there was no public enthusiasm for the man that has made the early history of that mining country romantic and famous all over the world."

Twain took the next day off, "laying around on the floor of his room all day reading and writing in his notebook and smoking."

On Monday, August 5, 1895, the group set out for the depot to catch the train to Missoula. On the platform, they spotted Mrs. Henry Ward Beecher, an old acquaintance who happened to be boarding the same train, traveling to Port Townsend to visit her son.

On arriving in the Garden City and settling in at the Florence Hotel, they learned that the commandant from Fort Missoula had invited them all to dine with him. The ladies accepted, but Twain was too tired and wanted to rest.

Mrs. Henry Ward Beecher, Senator Wilbur F. Sanders and Mark Twain in front of a train, Missoula, Montana, August 5, 1895. Photo courtesy Mark Twain Archive, Elmira College, Elmira, NY.

Twain's lecture that night at Missoula's Bennett Opera House drew praise from the local newspaper reviewer: "From the moment Mark Twain appeared before the footlights until the closing scene, the most respectful and highly appreciative attention was shown by the assemblage."

Twain recalled youthful days and lessons learned when he stole a watermelon, only to find it was still green. He reflected that a "right-minded boy" would promptly return the stolen property to its owner. So he did. "I told him he ought to be

TWAIN AT THE BENNETT

The World's Greatest Humorist Appears in Missoula.

HEARD BY A SPLENDID AUDIENCE

He Mixed Instruction Gratuitously With His Quaint Stories Last Night.

Missoulian, August 6, 1895.

ashamed of himself going around working off green watermelons in that way on people who had confidence in him ... and I made him give me a ripe one. Ever since that day I never stole another one ... (long pause) ... like that."

Major Pond wrote, "After the lecture, the meeting took the form of a social reception, and it was midnight before it broke up. The day has been one of delight to all of us."

Twain and his companions were to lunch the next day at Fort Missoula before their departure for Spokane. Twain rose early, deciding to leisurely walk out to the fort. The rest of the party waited for transportation (two army ambulances) sent by the commandant.

As the ambulances headed west, the party spotted a man – quite a distance away – signaling them. It was Twain. According to Pond's journal, Twain had "taken the wrong road, and after walking five or six miles on it, discovered his mistake, and was counter-marching when he saw our ambulance and ran across lots to meet us. He was tired – too tired to express disgust – and sat quietly inside the ambulance until we drove up to headquarters."

Pond described the band that greeted them as "one of the finest

Mark Twain and an unidentified officer at Fort Missoula, Montana, August 6, 1895. Photo courtesy Mark Twain Archive, Elmira College, Elmira, NY.

military bands in America," and said they "witnessed some fine drilling of the soldiers, and learned that for this kind of service the colored soldiers were more subordinate and submissive to rigid drill and discipline than white men, and that there were very few desertions from among them."

At 2:30 that afternoon, the Twain entourage boarded the westbound Northern Pacific, departing Missoula for Spokane. "Missoula feels honored by the courtesy of a visit from such a distinguished gentleman," wrote the *Missoulian*, "and the people hope that he will meet with the success which his splendid intellectual ability and pleasant personality merits." By the end of his "around the world" tour the next year, Twain had cleared his debt.

Chapter 6

AL JOLSON – AN INSTANT HIT IN MONTANA

Theater-goers in Butte and Missoula couldn't get enough of him. One 1917 newspaper review called him "an instantaneous hit, as frequent curtain calls and numerous personal talks to the audience proved. He said that he'd like to come back to Missoula, and, beyond a doubt, theater-going Missoula would be glad to welcome him again – even tonight."

Asa Yoelson, a Lithuanian immigrant, had just turned 31 when he came to Montana. Yet he already had nearly 20 years' experience in show business, having started as a child soon after his family arrived in America.

In the next few years, Asa would cement his name – and reputation

Jolson & Associates in Robinson Crusoe Jr., Bismarck Tribune, June 4, 1917.

– as "The World's Greatest Entertainer." Well, not his name; his stage name – Al Jolson.

In the four years that followed his Montana appearances, Jolson starred in New York musicals including George Gershwin's "Sinbad," which featured the song "Swanee," and later in "Bombo," where he sang "My Mammy." Jolson's recordings would sell millions of copies.

But in 1917, under contract with the New York Winter Garden, Jolson was a newly minted star – not yet a superstar – and was touring the country performing in a musical comedy called "Robinson Crusoe Jr." in places like Butte and Missoula.

The show was characterized as "frothy entertainment made up of a mixture of music, mirth and spectacular extravaganza," loosely based on the Robinson Crusoe story. There were some recognizable characters like Crusoe, the cannibals and Friday, played by Jolson.

In typical publicist puffery of the day, the females of the traveling company's Broadway Beauty Brigade were depicted as "bevies of bewilderingly bewitching blondes and brunettes – dozens of dainty, darling, dashing, deliriously delightful, Dresden-doll divinities – gorgeous galaxies of gushing, glittering, glorious, gladsome girlies."

Mostly, it was vintage vaudeville entertainment.

In addition to the Broadway Beauty Brigade, the huge traveling company of just over 200 included the Jockey Girls, wearing their racing caps, cravats, tight-fitting leggings and boots.

"The magnitude of the production," wrote the *Butte Daily Post*, "is suggested by the fact that a carload of special effects and the advance mechanical crew arrived (a day before) and have been at work ever since preparing the stage."

The performers and their support staff arrived the next day aboard a special train of 14 cars.

Jockey Girls ad. From the Butte Daily Post, June 9, 1917,

Despite the size of the troupe, the *Missoulian* newspaper's reviewer made it clear that "Jolson's support (cast) was good ... but Jolson was the show."

Based on the crowd size, "it was exactly that for which Missoula had been waiting ... for there was not a seat unsold – or unoccupied – last evening."

AL JOLSON GREAT HIT WITH CAPACITY HOUSE

Bright Winter Garden Offering Delights Large Missoula Audience.

SHOW IS REMARKABLE

Musical Comedy Has Both Harmony and Wit, an Unusual Circumstance.

Headline from The Daily Missoulian, June 16, 1917.

The show had only an outline of a script. For the most part, it depended on Jolson himself guiding the audience from one bit to the next and occasionally taking time to chat directly with the locals about "everything from dry laws to his wife."

In addition to the advance advertising for the show itself, Montana newspapers carried another ad – this one from Jolson's label, Columbia Records, hyping his "latest and biggest hits."

Those recordings included one featured in the 1917 touring show titled "Where Did Robinson Crusoe Go with Friday on Saturday Night?" (You can listen to the record on YouTube).

The label also bragged of its recording technology, which reproduced Jolson's voice "with the same mirror-like brilliant fidelity" as its recordings of operas and orchestras.

The Winter Garden-Robinson Crusoe 139-performance tour was declared "one of the most successful tours in American theatrical history," by a trade magazine.

For all his success, Jolson's career had its rough spots. Some criticized his use of blackface as racist. Others noted his mistreatment as a Jew, especially by Lee and Jacob Shubert, whose theatrical empire included New York's Winter Garden.

John Kenric in his book, *Musical Theatre: A History*, pointed out that, on the one hand the Shuberts built Jolson a special runway so the star could "deliver solos right in the middle of the audience."

On the other hand, while praising Jolson in public, they "subjected him to the same strong-arm tactics they used with everyone else." Fanny Brice described it this way: "It took the Shuberts to figure out a new way to kill Jews."

By the mid-1920s, Jolson and the Shuberts were hardly getting along. That led Jolson to hook up with Warner Brothers and a new way to reach his audience: film.

The silent era was ending, and Jolson's starring role as "The Jazz Singer," helped trigger the conversion to sound movies at theaters across the country.

Jolson's final tour came in 1950 – a grueling 40 shows in two weeks – performing for troops in the Korean War.

Perhaps it was the strain of the tour – no one could be sure – but Jolson died of a heart attack just weeks after the Korean shows. He was awarded the Medal of Merit, posthumously, by Defense Secretary George Marshall.

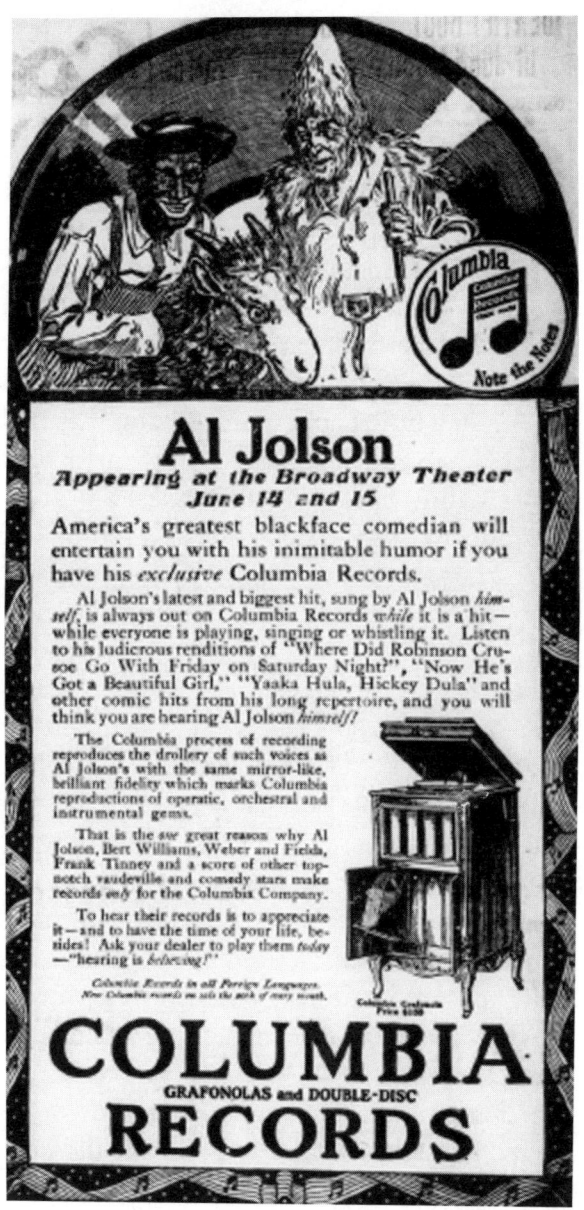

Ad for Jolson & Columbia Records, from Butte Daily Post, June 12, 1917.

Chapter 7

MARY GLEIM
– QUEEN OF THE "MIDWAY PLAISANCE" –

Mary Gleim is among Missoula's most colorful historical characters. So much has been written about her, I hesitate to go down this road, except for the fact that the details of her downfall are usually glossed over in a few sentences. They deserve so much more.

First, a little background. Gleim was Irish, educated in England and fluent in several languages. She was a businesswoman when women weren't allowed to own businesses. She and her husband John moved to Missoula in 1888. Using John as a "front," Gleim amassed considerable wealth from real estate and importing/smuggling everything from lace goods to opium.

> As the result of a row between those ever interesting rival Midway landlords, Bobby Burns and Mrs. Gleim, the former has been arrested for drawing a deadly weapon and threatening to perforate the precious hide of the female Sandow.
>
> *Newspaper clipping from the Missoulian, March 7, 1894.*

But her place in history will always be as Missoula's "Madam of Front Street," operating eight brothels ... er ... "boarding houses." Her chief rival in the "boarding house business" was Bobby Burns.

Neither Burns nor Gleim were to be messed with; both had explosive personalities. Gleim, the size of a grizzly bear with the temperament of a pit bull on a bad day, was arrested one time "for drawing a revolver on Billy Hawkes and threatening to convert him into a dashing young angel."

Burns, about the same time, was arrested for "drawing a deadly weapon and threatening to perforate the precious hide" of Mrs. Gleim.

Over the years, it seemed Missoula's most notorious bad girl could get away with anything. In an era when local judges had little tolerance for lawbreakers (vagrants were sentenced to 30 days on the county's woodpile and hog thieves got seven years in the state pen), Gleim skated.

In one incident, the 300-pound madam assaulted two priests at their residence after they failed to appreciate her advice on how to run the Catholic church. "She attempted to tear their clothes and demolish the furniture," reported the *Missoulian*. Then upon leaving, she attacked her hack (cab) driver.

On the occasions when she was dragged into court, she would routinely spew vile epithets at the judge, attorneys and witnesses. When a lawyer objected to one such tantrum, she "squared herself off at him and dared him to do anything."

In virtually every case, the shady lady would either be acquitted or ordered to pay a small fine. Even when fined, she would promptly appeal and, usually, win.

The story of Mary's downfall began innocently enough on January 30, 1894. One of the Missoula newspapers carried a short item which read, "The charming Madame Gleim departed today on a visit to California's Midwinter Midway and will not return for several weeks, much to the satisfaction of the many denizens of her neighborhood, who always breathe easier when she is away."

What no one knew was that Gleim had hired some thugs to (literally) blow up the competition while she was conveniently out of town. The *Missoulian's* story on the incident is a journalistic gem:

> The lady took a hack soon after supper and went to pay some visits. On her road home she stopped at the residence of Father Diomedi and the other Catholic priests and while there manifested a desire to act as an advisory board for the entire Catholic church. She was, of course, kindly received, but when she found that some of her advice would not be immediately followed grew abusive, and ended by making an assault on Father Neal and Brother Meggazzine. She attempted to tear their clothes and demolish the furniture, and when she found that they did nothing but retire and leave the field to her she left in disgust. It then occurred to her that she had got herself into trouble and that if the hack had not stopped there it would not have happened. Accordingly she assaulted the hack driver. At last she was arrested by Officers Keim and Elletson and placed in jail, bonds being refused. The Fathers were loth to swear out complaints against the lady, but finally did so, and she will be tried before Judge Evans tomorrow at 2 o'clock.

Newspaper Clipping, Audra Bowman Research Room, Missoula City Library.

"*February 12, 1894 – A portion of Bobby Burns residence, on the bank of the river in the rear of one of the W. Front St. palaces of sin, took a trip skyward about 3:15 this morning being greatly augmented in its desire for aerial fame by a stick of dynamite which had been placed under the little shack, by some person or persons who evidently have but little love for the aforementioned 'Bobby.'*

"*Dynamite has its peculiarities and to this fact Burns probably owes his life. The force of the discharge was evidently not what was expected but was sufficient to tear out the lower portions of the building and completely wreck the contents of the room in which Burns was sleeping*

Backside of Front Street buildings, circa 1894, in area of explosion. University of Montana Archives & Special Collections.

at the time and a tin wash basin, which was standing outside a door of the room, was blown a distance of 60 feet and lodged in the branches of a tree at the edge of the river.

A FIENDISH ACT.

A Local Vaillant Fires a Stick of Dynamite.

IT WRECKS BOBBY BURNS' HOUSE

A Midnight Deed Which Will Go Hard On the Perpetrator If Detected.

Headline from the Missoulian, February 12, 1894.

"There is no clue to the perpetrator of the outrage, though Burns himself claims that he has been expecting something of the sort for some time and believes the guilty party to be a neighbor of his. The affair is the talk of the town."

Missoula's other paper, the *Western Democrat*, reported the only reason Burns wasn't killed was that the culprits, in the dark of night, blew up the wrong building: "The investigation showed that the rear end of the building next to the one he occupied had been destroyed. The two houses were nearly alike and there appears to be no doubt that the fiend perpetrating the outrage intended the destruction of Mr. Burns and his property by dynamite."

Burns promptly offered a $500 reward for any information, and though it seemed apparent to everyone what really happened, months went by with no arrests.

The city did, however, put on a good show of cracking down on the "worthless elements" of Missoula's "Midway Plaisance" (a phrase appropriated from the recent Chicago World Exposition). The *Missoulian* reported, "The officers have again commenced a raid on that idle, worthless and despicable class of humanity, known to the community as pimps or secretaries."

Finally, in August, a grand jury indicted Gleim and two accomplices, Pat Mason, a "worthless sort of fellow around town," and Pvt. William Reed, a "colored soldier" of the 25th infantry at Fort Missoula, for attempted murder. The three were immediately jailed, but Gleim was allowed a quantity of booze to drink while in the slammer. That led to more trouble.

"It was a bad night; the quantity of booze allowed her had run out only too soon and she took occasion to vent her spleen on a fellow prisoner," according to one account. "When brought into court this morning 'Mother' Gleim ... declined to permit the court to appoint counsel for her and took occasion to express herself regarding some members of the local legal fraternity in – to say the least – a decidedly unprofessional way."

While awaiting trial, Gleim (accompanied by a deputy) was allowed out of jail by day to conduct business about town.

At the first of the trials, in early September 1894, Patrick James Mason was convicted of

Clipping from the Western Democrat, February 18, 1894.

> There was also indictments returned against Mary Gleim, the Empress of hell's half acre, Patrick Mason and William Reed, for assault with intent to commit murder, charging that on the morning of February 13, Patrick Mason, aided and incited by Mary Gleim and William Reed, did place a stick of giant powder under the house of "Bobby" Burns on the Midway and blew the house into smithereens. Mrs. Gleim was in California at the time the dastardly act took place, but it is claimed by the state that she was the instigator of the affair and left for California before the raise took place.

Gleim indicted, Western Democrat, August 14, 1894.

43

assault with intent to murder Bobby Burns. Judge Frank Woody described the crime as a "cowardly" act and, noting that dynamiting had become all too common and must be stopped, sentenced Mason to the maximum of 14 years in the state pen.

Next would be the trial of the soldier, William Reed. But, on a last-minute motion by the county attorney (in an apparent plea deal), the case against Reed was dismissed, so he could testify against Mary Gleim.

The courthouse was packed for Gleim's trial, but the atmosphere was subdued. From the minute the "Madam" was arrested, Judge Frank Woody made it clear he wasn't about to let his courtroom be turned into the usual Gleim circus. He even threatened local attorneys with contempt if they signed the defendant's bail bond papers.

The defense team, made up of high-profile lawyers from Helena, was ready – objecting to everything. They challenged potential jurors. When they ran out of peremptory challenges, and the jury was seated, they challenged the jury as a whole. They objected to witnesses. They objected to testimony. They even objected to the prosecution's closing argument.

But Judge Woody would have none of it.

Witnesses, including "ladies of the night," recounted the February explosion and Bobby Burns' brush with death. The defense tried to establish that one such witness, Nellie Harding, was a habitual "morphine eater," but Judge Woody said he didn't believe that affected her credibility.

> Efforts have been made by the defense to secure a change of venue on the ground that nearly everybody in this community is prejudiced against the woman who has permitted herself to be drawn into this entanglement, but the proposition has been rejected by Judge Woody, and unless some good cause for a further continuance can be shown, the trial of the case will be proceeded with.

Defense efforts for a change of venue denied, Missoulian, September 12, 1894.

Chester Newgate, a former Gleim employee and the main prosecution witness, told of overhearing Gleim and convicted dynamiter Pat Mason as they conspired to "rid the community" of Burns. Newgate claimed Gleim tried to get Mason to either poison Burns or kill him with a crowbar. He also said Gleim left a gun with him, instructing him "if Mason called for it, give it to him."

The defense objected to allowing Newgate to testify at all, asserting he was a convicted felon who had blown up a house in Colorado in an attempt to kill a woman and her daughter. They asked for time to investigate the matter, but Judge Woody overruled their objection and refused to delay the trial.

Another witness, John Woods, testified that Gleim told him, "Burns ought to be blown up; they ought to hang him; she said he had killed a Chinaman."

Pvt. Reed, Mason's partner in crime but now a prosecution witness, claimed Mason told him Madam Gleim was the "head pusher" in the scheme.

Gleim took the stand in her own defense, denying everything. After all, she was in San Francisco when it happened and besides it was just a big conspiracy. But nothing seemed to go her way.

Bill of Exceptions from the Gleim trial, Missoula County Records Center.

Despite the Gleim team's strenuous objections, Prosecutor Thomas C. Marshall, Esq., in his closing argument, painted Mary Gleim as a woman who "never had any money in her life that was not tainted with crime," and after nine hours of deliberation, the jury found her guilty.

The next day, Gleim was allowed to go about town (in the company of a deputy) to wrap up her business affairs, as the courthouse filled with locals, jockeying for position to watch the sentencing. Given the defendant's outbursts in the past, quite a show was anticipated. But it didn't happen.

When Judge Woody asked Gleim if she had anything to say, she calmly replied, "Not a word, proceed." So the judge did. "Then it is the sentence of this court," declared Woody, "that you, Mary E. Gleim, be imprisoned at hard labor in the Western Montana Penitentiary at Deer Lodge for a term of 14 years."

At that, someone in the audience shouted, "Don't get excited, it's all right." Gleim turned to one of her attorneys and said, "Excited, who's excited? There is nothing to get excited about in a little matter like this. The people in this courtroom are more excited than I." And with that, she was off to Deer Lodge.

The portly madam is said to have arrived at prison fashionably dressed. Once settled in, she continued to conduct some business, deeding to her husband, John, "for a consideration of love and affection," some building lots in Missoula's McCormick addition, along with other parcels.

As she quickly learned, however – in prison, she was no longer in charge; no longer the "Queen of the Badlands;" no longer feared by all. Another female inmate, sent to the pen from Missoula, severely beat and stabbed Gleim in the yard one day.

Meantime, her team of attorneys compiled a 30-page "list of exceptions" (appeal).* In little over a year, they won a new trial for Gleim in which she prevailed. By early 1896, Gleim was back in Missoula, living at one of her properties, the Star Lodging House, where she promptly assaulted one of her boarders, "French Emma," with a beer bottle, and proclaimed there weren't enough officers in town to arrest her!

Mary Gleim died on February 22, 1914, leaving a substantial estate. Arthur L. Stone wrote her obituary for the *Missoulian*: "She was a relentless hater and during the days when she figured so prominently in the battles of a wide open town, she fought some hard battles. These were real battles too. She fought physically and was able to handle any man who ever went against her, even when he was clothed in official authority.

MARY GLEIM DIES QUEER LIFE ENDS

Headline in the Missoulian upon Mary Gleim's death. February 23, 1914

"Hers was a strange life. Its chapters would make a wonderful book. But it is not likely that they will ever be written. Some of her adventures she had related herself, but as a whole the story of her career was a sealed volume."

#

Author's Note: *Unfortunately, very little verbatim testimony from Gleim's attempted murder trial was transcribed, either in the local newspapers or official court records. There appears to be no transcript* *of the proceedings. If one was made, it was not maintained. Most of the witness quotes used in this story came from the "list of exceptions" filed with the court, and preserved at the Missoula County Records Center.*

Chapter 8

END OF THE BADLANDS – THE NIGHT THE RED LIGHTS WENT OUT

February 1, 1917, was the night the lights went out in Missoula. "The 'line' ceased to exist at 12:01 o'clock this morning," reported the local paper. "The demise was quiet. The police were on hand...but they weren't needed. Most of the women had packed their belongings and decamped" the day before.

RED LIGHTS TURNED OUT

Restricted District Closed Without Trouble; Inmates Leaving.

Missoulian, February 1, 1917.

Samuel Clarence Ford had been elected Montana Attorney General the previous fall, campaigning that he would strongly enforce the – until then – largely ignored laws outlawing prostitution. Upon taking office he sent letters to county and city officials advising them "to take (action) against the managers and proprietors of residence property, hotels, rooming houses and and the like which may be occupied in violation of the law."

When will we dwellers in the twentieth century come to the conclusion that if to deal in women is bad, to tax and license the same women is not strictly genteel?

How proud we are of the enlightened public sentiment which guides our governmental action! How humble we ought to be rather, when we really achieve a little of such sentiment— enough of it to slap Sam Ford on the back and say "We're with you!"

———o———

Dillon Tribune, January 12, 1917.

Missoula Mayor H. T. Wilkinson and Missoula County Attorney Fred Angevine quickly issued a joint statement declaring that all prostitution laws would be strictly enforced and that the red light district would be closed.

Specifically, the law said, "Every person who keeps any disorderly house, or any house for the purpose of assignation or prostitution, or any house of public resort, by which the peace, comfort or decency of the immediate neighborhood is habitually disturbed, or who keeps any inn in a disorderly manner, and every person who lets any apartment or tenement, knowing it is to be used for the purpose of assignation or prostitution, is guilty of a misdemeanor."

For decades the infamous houses along west Front Street, with names like the "Last Chance" and the "Star" lodging house had not only been tolerated but produced thousands of dollars in taxes and fees for the city coffers. The estimate for one year was $15,000.

Known variously as the Midway Plaisance, the Bad Lands or the Restricted District, the area was the site of drunken brawls, drug dens and mysterious deaths by poison and other means. One judge was quoted as saying, "This city has acquired a reputation in this respect as bad, or worse than any other town in the state."

The local paper recounted, "In the old days of honkatonks and open gambling it was a wild, vigorous institution. Murder and robbery were frequent, for booze flowed free all along the 'line,' and nothing was barred." The "line" was a reference to all of west Front street and most all of west Main, where the streets were "lined" with houses of ill repute.

By the afternoon of January 31, 1917 – in the hours before the crackdown, expecting law enforcement raids – women from the district began packing their bags. Rumors on the streets were that many of the women would just move to other rooming houses or private residences, but city officials were "inclined to believe that the danger of promiscuity has been exaggerated." No one really believed that the crackdown would totally do away with the evil, but most agreed the law ought be be enforced.

For about a month, things were quiet. But in early March, 1917 "a former inmate of the resorts," Hazel Hall, was arrested and fined $50. The fine was set aside on Hazel's promise that she would leave town within 24 hours. At the time, the police chief was quoted as saying, "To my knowledge there are only four or five former residents of the restricted district in the city at the present time. Two of those are running rooming houses and carrying on a legitimate business in a manner occasioning no complaint. The others are conducting themselves in a proper manner so far as we have been able to learn."

(Section 8, Page 5, Laws Twelfth Legislative Assembly)

Section 8.—Any person who shall knowingly accept, receive, levy, or appropriate any money or other valuable thing without consideration, from the proceeds or earnings of any woman engaged in prostitution shall be deemed guilty of a felony and, on conviction thereof, shall be punishable by imprisonment in the state prison for a period of not less than two years nor more than twenty years, or by fine of not less than one thousand dollars nor more than five thousand dollars, or by both such fine and imprisonment. Any such acceptance, receipt, levy, or appropriation of such money or valuable thing shall upon any proceeding or trial for violation of this section be presumptive evidence of lack of consideration.

*Mineral Independent,
February 1, 1917.*

That a murder was not committed early this morning on the midway plaisance is probably not due to the murderous looking weapon that was employed by one of the participants in an all around fight among the denizens of that district, nor to the evident bloodthirstiness of Miss Bebe Campbell, who occupied a position at the working end of the miniature cannon.

*Weekly Missoulian,
July 18, 1894.*

But a few months later three women were arrested along with with a couple of soldiers at the European hotel on Railroad street, exposing the "shocking condition of immorality in militia guard camps near Missoula." Two of the women, who had an "affection for khaki," were allowed to leave town rather than being fined. The third was handed over to a probation officer.

In at least one case, though, a young woman from Butte's restricted district, turned the tables on those who would have her locked up. She hired a lawyer and brought suit for "damages for the loss of her soul." She claimed, "I have lost my soul and I want to sue for its value (explaining) that several years ago she was allowed to go to cafes and dances where liquor was sold, although only 16 years old. She blames this fact for her downfall and says the city and county government are responsible." It's unlikely her claim was successful, but we don't know. Sad to say, no follow-up story could be found on the outcome of her case.

Clipping from the Missoulian, February 2, 1917 – Lawsuit for soul.

Viola, a former inmate of the restricted district of Butte, has engaged counsel to bring suit for damages for the loss of her soul. "I have lost my soul and want to sue for its value," she explained.

As for the bigger picture, the statewide crackdown on prostitution proved extremely effective. The long tolerated "restricted districts" disappeared from Montana cities and towns, in many cases – like Missoula – literally overnight. But, the stories from that period remain a colorful part of the state's history. A handful of the most famous buildings used as brothels back in the day, still remain: Big Dorothy's in Helena, the Dumas in Butte and Madam Mary Gleim's West Front Street building in Missoula, dating to 1893. Nearly 100 years later, in 1990, the Gleim building at 265 West Front Street, was added to the National Register of Historic Places.

Chapter 9

SALOONS – 'SEGAR' SMOKE, STALE WHISKEY AND A FRESH CROISSANT

Alcohol has been a part of human society for eons – perhaps as far back as Neolithic times, about 10,000 BCE. All along, it has generated both commerce and controversy.

Western lore and Montana history are positively steeped in booze. After all, a town wasn't really a town until it had a saloon.

Montana's first newspaper (*Montana Post*, Virginia City, 1864) encouraged readers to "go and see the boys" at the Head-Quarters Saloon and "strengthen (your) inner man." At the same time, it duly reported the death of one fella who succumbed to "exposure caused by intemperance ... another of rum's victims."

Saloon advertising filled many of Montana's early papers. They're fun to read. A couple of the best come from Deer Lodge City's newspaper, the *Weekly Independent* in 1867.

> FOUND DEAD.—A man was found in our city yesterday morning dead. An inquest was held on the body, and the verdict, as we learn, was death by exposure caused by intemperance. We did not learn the name of the deceased, but note this case as another of "rum's victims." He was decently buried by the authorities.
>
> *Montana Post, 1864.*

The ad for "Wilson's California Bakery" is unremarkable until you reach a line that causes a double-take. Conveniently attached to the bakery is a "magnificent bar supplied with the finest kinds of liquors and segars (sic)." The ad goes on to say, "Billy is always on hand to attend to the most refined imbibers – or 'any other man.'"

Ah, the aroma of Deer Lodge City in 1867: "Segar" smoke, stale whiskey and a fresh croissant.

In the same issue, the Bed Rock Saloon in Philipsburg assured readers that its proprietor, Newton Dickinson, would always be "on hand to attend to strangers personally." Apparently drinking men, especially strangers, needed a lot of attention.

Missoula had a robust drinking scene in its early days. Besides the notorious sanctums of the prescribed district, there were respectable saloons galore.

The Capital Beer Hall made its name by serving fresh rabbit stew to its customers. When owner Andy Schilling wasn't hunting local game, he was importing the ingredients for his famous clam chowder, "the most palatable dish ever set before the bulging eyes of hungry humanity."

In the late 1890s, Al Holbert and Warren Shopp reopened Missoula's mothballed Headquarters Saloon (seems to be a popular saloon name). The *Missoulian* declared it "a howling success." There was a turkey banquet and a live orchestra. The revelry lasted until well past midnight.

The Toothsome Rabbit.
Joe Schilling, the nimrod of the Capital beer hall has just returned from a rabbit hunting trip loaded down with cotton-tail and other kinds of tall rabbits and the menu at this popular resort will consist of rabbit stews for the next few days. Andy Schilling, the proprietor, extends a cordial invitation to the public to drop in and sample his chef's art in this respect. j26t2

Rabbit Stew, ad in Missoulian, 1864.

Drink more pure beer

The nations that drink the most of it suffer the least from nervousness and dyspepsia.

But the slightest taint of impurity ruins its healthfulness. Be sure you get pure beer.

This Schlitz ad, circa 1914, urged viewers to drink more beer.

If you were to believe the newspaper advertising of the day, imbibing was good for your health. Schlitz encouraged you to "drink more pure beer." After all, the "nations that drink the most of it suffer the least from nervousness and dyspepsia. It will not cause biliousness – it gives you the good without the harm."

Duffy's Pure Malt Whiskey claimed to "improve the digestion and assimilation of food and give tone and vitality to every organ of the body." And the salubrious claims didn't end there. Why, it was said to be useful in alleviating coughs, colds and asthma. It even claimed to prevent and relieve pneumonia and malaria!

Is it 5 o'clock, yet?

Alcohol sales and saloon taxes proved to be a financial boon to

Duffy's Pure Malt Whiskey
For Medicinal Use

Savannah Morning News, Georgia, 1899.

cities like Missoula. For example, in 1894, the annual municipal financial report listed income just under $22,000. Most of that came from general taxes, but the second largest source was saloon and gambling licenses (nearly $2,000).

There was opposition to all this boozing, to be sure.

In 1866, the Territorial Legislature passed a law outlawing gaming, dance houses and hurdy-gurdy houses on "the Lord's Day," with scofflaws facing fines and jail time. But lawmakers didn't ban liquor or saloon operations.

In 1873, there was a movement to establish a "Sunday Law" in the Territory, prohibiting business of any kind to promote "better observance of the Sabbath."

Gambl'g houses and faro t'bls	14	560 00
Hacks and transfer wagons	17	85 00
Hawkers		
Hotels and restaurants	25	75 00
Laundries	17	85 00
Lodging houses	4	12 00
Livery and feed stables	12	60 00
Liquor dealers, wholesale	8	72 00
Merchants	144	735 00
Peddlers	12	12 00
Professions	6	9 00
Pawnbrokers	6	90 00
Saloons	99	1237 50

Missoula city financial report for 1894.

The *Weekly Missoulian*, while agreeing Sunday should be a day of rest, argued such a law would never be enforced. "Better have no laws at all than have laws that are constantly violated with impunity."

The paper pointed out that in the local mining camps, Sunday was the only day men had to make most of their purchases and there likely wouldn't be a soul "who would make a complaint against the merchants and saloon keepers" who did business. In fact, it argued: "Close up stores by this act, and the owners will sell goods out of the rear. Close up saloons, and men will buy liquor by the bottle and make beasts of themselves."

THE SUNDAY QUESTION.

The question of a Sunday law now being agitated by the press of the Territory, and petitions are being circulated, asking that the legislature pass an act for the better observance of the Sabbath day. We do not know what the sentiments of the people are on this subject, but we have our views, and will express them. We desire to see the sabbath observed as a day of rest;

Weekly Missoulian, 1873.

In the late 1890s, Stevensville's paper, the *North West Tribune*, carried a weekly column on its front pages authored by the Women's Christian Temperance Union. The articles decried "the brutal murder of helpless women and children and the demoniacal deeds of rum-crazed fiends resulting from the licensed liquor traffic."

The Salvation Army did its part to try to save Montana's poor souls from alcohol's "cesspool of sin," but their soldiers were often "jeered by men and boys old enough to know better." The *Missoulian* rather weakly admonished the hecklers, saying the Salvationists were at least "entitled to the respect of the community, even though they may be denied its support."

As for me, I'll follow the wisdom of Ben Franklin, who was known to say, "In wine there is wisdom, in beer there is freedom, in water there is bacteria." But let's not fight over it, OK?

W. C. T. U. COLUMN.

IS CIVILIZATION A LIE.

The brutal murder of helpless women and children and the demoniacal deeds of rum crazed fiends resulting from the licenced liquor traffic, have in no wise diminished during the past few weeks. Every day adds new horrors to the sickening record

W.C.T.U column from the North West Tribune, 1894.

Chapter 10

GUNFIGHT ON HIGGINS BRIDGE
TRAIN CONDUCTOR & DENTIST NEAR DEATH

"Between the miniature clouds of smoke could be seen the upright forms of two men, emptying their revolvers at each other as quickly as triggers could be pulled." In seconds, the gunfight on the Higgins Avenue bridge was over, but it had been months in the making.

In late 1893 continuing into 1894, hurtful anonymous letters were circulated in Missoula, casting aspersions and causing considerable angst. The targets were members of the city's "swell set," the well-to-do of society.

The newspapers of the day did not specify the contents of the letters since doing so would further injure the reputations of the targeted individuals, but they did call out the malevolent writers in an effort to end the practice.

The *Anaconda Standard* in December 1893 noted, "There is a general complaint against the rowdyism and lawlessness of a number of young men about town who are in the habit of creating disturbances in public meetings and otherwise bringing disgrace upon the reputation of Missoula as a law-abiding community."

> IT'S A NUISANCE.
> Fresh Young Men Who Continue to Indulge in Vulgar Practical Jokes.
>
> MISSOULA, Dec. 6.—There is a general complaint against the rowdyism and lawlessness of a number of young men about town who are in the habit of creating disturbances in public meetings and otherwise bringing disgrace upon the reputation of Missoula as a law-abiding community. The practice of sending anonymous letters, previously referred to in the STANDARD, was bad enough, without having further outrages perpetrated upon public decency, but there seems to be no end to the schemes of annoyance which are devised and carried out here in Missoula.

Anaconda Standard, December 7, 1893.

The paper continued, "The practice of sending anonymous letters, previously referred to in the *Standard*, was bad enough, without having further outrages perpetrated upon public decency, but there seems to be no end to the schemes of annoyance which are devised and carried out here in Missoula."

The consequences would soon be significant, and near fatal.

In early 1894, the *Missoulian* called for an immediate stop to the practice: "the community will be surprised to know that the perpetrators lay claim to be called gentlemen, (God save the mark!) and are supposed to occupy responsible business positions and have also been accorded social standing. Do they imagine that reputable banking or mercantile concerns would employ or do business with men who are so handy with the pen? Hardly! The verdict of the community is more apt to be, that a man who would commit a social forgery like this latest effort of these 'gentlemen' would need small temptation to wield the same facile pen – using somebody else's name – on the back of a note, check or other negotiable paper."

The public joined the call to end the practice, including one person who penned a letter to the editor, saying "it is (hoped) the infamous practice of anonymous letter writing has also ceased and the blackmailer, who seeks to retaliate for some fancied injury, has been laid away on the shelf. The city of Missoula has been sufficiently disgraced and dishonored, and even to the extent of frightening people from this community has the practice been carried on."

> the shelf. The city of Missoula has been sufficiently disgraced and dishonored, and even to the extent of frightening people from this community has the practice been carried on. Ladies have been insulted, individuals maligned and, in some instances, have efforts been made to break up happy homes. Persons, without sufficient nerve to make known their identity, have endeavored to levy a system of blackmail, and, failing in which, have sought other methods of "getting even" on innocent persons whom they fancy have wronged them. I say, Mr. Editor, I believe that all of this business has been stopped; at least I think it has, and for all of which the people of this fair but damnably handicapped city should be thankful.
>
> *Letter to Editor, Missoulian, 1894.*

Just a few months later, though, in late April 1894, anonymous letter-writing combined with an overdue dental bill for $19 brought two highly respected Missoulians face to face in a near-deadly shootout on the Higgins Avenue bridge.

"Shortly after 6:30 o'clock last evening, the reports of rapid pistol firing in the direction of the south end of the Higgins Avenue Bridge (were heard)" the *Missoulian* reported. "(B)etween the miniature clouds of smoke could be seen the upright forms of two men, emptying their revolvers at each other as quickly as triggers could be pulled."

The paper continued "As a consequence of the fusilade, Jack Doudell, conductor of the Bitter Root branch trains and one of the oldest and best known employees of the Northern Pacific on the Rocky Mountain division, is lying at his pretty little home in South Fourth Street

THEY CERTAINLY SHOT TO KILL.

Dr. Fred Ellis and Jack Doudell Meet on the Highway.

A FUSILADE OF BULLETS

Fast and Furious Gun Fighting in Which Neither Flinched a Particle.

Missoulian, April 27, 1894.

hovering between life and death, a bullet lodged in his right lung and his chances of recovery decidedly in the minority, and Dr. Fred F. Ellis, the well-known dentist of the Higgins block, is under the care of three physicians at his residence, at the extreme southern terminus of Higgins Avenue, with three bullet holes in his body, the extent of his injuries not having yet been fully determined."

The simmering dispute between the two could be traced back to anonymous, disparaging rumors circulating about town targeting Doudell – rumors he believed were the doing of Dr. Ellis.

> The MISSOULIAN sold like hot cakes last night, an exceedingly large extra edition was run off but the supply was insufficient to meet the demand.
>
> Go to church tomorrow and pray that peace may once more reign supreme throughout this fair little city.
>
> *Missoulian, April 28, 1894.*

Ellis told reporters the next day: "This trouble with Doudell has been brewing for some time. Just one month ago today, Doudell came to my office and without making any explanation, placed his hand in his hip pocket and said, 'Ellis if I were to do the proper thing I would shoot you down in your tracks like a dog.' I started to expostulate with him when he warned me if I said another word he would kill me then and there."

Ellis continued: "Naturally enough, I at once subsided and he took his departure, but not until he had remarked that he would investigate the matter, which he had failed to explain to me, and if he found out to his satisfaction that I was guilty, he would send a bullet through my heart. I left town the next morning on business and did not return for two or three days."

It was "presumed, by those who should best be in a position to know," according to the *Missoulian,* "that Doudell was the recipient of one of the numerous infamous anonymous letters which a short time ago were so generally circulated throughout the city, the contents of which were of a nature calculated to bring about an intense hatred for his former friend, Dr. Ellis."

Doudell apparently snapped that April evening when he stopped for his mail on the way home to find a past-due notice from a collection agent, regarding a $19 dental bill owed Ellis for work on Mrs. Doudell. When he sighted Dr. Ellis on the Higgins Bridge, he grabbed his gun and set out to confront the man.

Doudell (according to Ellis) told the doctor's companions, "Here you men, step aside, I want to pay this (expletive) bill I owe him," and went for his gun.

Reporters tried to get a reaction to the claim from Doudell, but "the wounded man's condition is such that any attempt at conversation is considered inadvisable by his physicians."

As the two men recovered from their wounds, Missoula County Attorney Iullus Greenleaf Denny (his first name was pronounced EYE'-you-luss) charged both men with assault with a deadly weapon with intent to commit murder. But by mid-August 1894, Denny admitted the chances of getting a conviction were near zero since each party "would swear to a state of facts totally at variance with the other," so he reduced the charges to simple assault.

> Complaints charging both Doudell and Ellis with an assault to commit murder will be filed by County Attorney Denny late this afternoon, when the men will be placed under bonds and the guards removed.
>
> *Missoulian, April 28, 1894.*

Judge Frank Woody, according to the *Missoulian*, "was inclined to agree with the county attorney in his views and believed that both parties to the South Side battle had learned a wholesome lesson. He believed that henceforth the gentlemen would be content to remain as peaceable, law-abiding citizens and that they had experienced a great sufficiency of their peculiar 'target practice.'"

The two were fined $50 and court costs.

> Shortly after the opening of court this morning, County Attorney Denny asked leave to practically withdraw the informations against John Doudell and Dr. Fred F. Ellis, each charged with an assault with a deadly weapon with intent to commit murder and that the defendants be permitted to plead guilty to charges of simple assault. Mr. Denny went on to say that he had made a careful study of these cases; there were no eye witnesses to the famous duel other than the principals, themselves, and the members of their respective families. Each would swear to a state of facts totally at variance with the other and a conviction under the circumstances would be practically out of the question.
>
> *Missoulian, April, 1894.*

Chapter 11

MURDER OF A NATIVE SON

Some say it started with the explosion of a lamp. Whatever the cause, at about 6 o'clock on the night of August 16, 1892, fire swept through the Blue Front Saloon on West Front Street in Missoula.

"In a space of time that might be counted in seconds, the Chinese laundry to the east had caught fire, also the laundry to the west and the blacksmith shop of Deschamps & Hayes and the laundry and the Star and Crescent, the frame building just west," reported the local paper.

Next to go was the Johnson & Daly livery stable. Then the inferno jumped the street, torching a private residence, a secondhand store, a tailor shop, a pawn shop and a restaurant.

Only when it reached an as-yet-unfinished brick building did the conflagration slow. Still, the Eddy block, the McCormick property and the Florence Hotel "seemed doomed."

> **A Big Fire in Missoula—Maurice Higgins Shot.**
>
> A disastrous fire broke out in Missoula last Sunday evening, destroying $42,900 worth of property. The principal losses were the Louvre building, Eclipse stables, Mrs. Kate McCormick's residence and the Rogers House. The fire started in the Blue Front saloon on Front street and soon everything in that vicinity was in flames. It was with great difficulty that the Missoula hotel was saved. The fire is supposed to have been of incendiary origin.
>
> *The Montanian,*
> *August 19, 1892.*

Miraculously, a sudden change in wind direction allowed firefighters to get the upper hand in the early morning hours. "Without their noble efforts," wrote the *Missoulian* newspaper, "the loss would have been twenty times greater."

While the fire was costly, it was not without its benefits. The buildings burned were described as "of the nature that ought to have been pulled down a year ago, as (they were) a constant menace to valuable and substantial buildings."

The local paper declared "satisfaction in knowing that the vacant ground cannot be again encumbered with wooden shacks (and) ... is now safe, barring accident, from fire for a long time to come."

About 4 o'clock in the morning, as smoke hung over the city, 23-year-old Maurice Higgins, a volunteer on the fire brigade and member of one of Missoula's wealthiest families (including C.P. Higgins, the city's founder), took a break after spending the night battling the blaze.

Another young man, Paul Goldenbogen, watched the dwindling fire a few steps away in front of the Mascot Theater. Both were about to become part of "one of the saddest tragedies in the history of Missoula."

Goldenbogen, who had earlier witnessed a man steal some items from a local store, observed the man again and confronted him. Words were exchanged and the thief, later identified as a drifter named John Burns, pulled a revolver and shot Goldenbogen in the left arm.

Maurice G. Higgins as a boy. Courtesy UM Archives & Special Collections.

"Goldenbogen staggered from the shot and reeled toward the group (including Higgins), when Burns shot again, the bullet missing Paul and striking Maurice Higgins in the center of the forehead," according to a press account.

Higgins was rushed to his family residence; Goldenbogen to the Sisters hospital. Both suffered what appeared to be mortal wounds.

Goldenbogen, from his hospital bed, identified the shooter as John Burns and Sheriff William H. Houston quickly apprehended the drifter. Townspeople were "much worked up over the affair." Some began talking about lynching the murderer, but cooler heads prevailed.

Maurice Higgins' brother, George, left immediately for Victoria, B.C., to bring their mother back to Missoula to see "her favorite son." But at 3:30 that afternoon, young Maurice Higgins died.

A month later, before a packed courtroom, the trial commenced. The judge had to repeatedly order the sheriff to make the spectators get back behind the railing and sit down. The defendant, on the other hand, appeared cool and collected.

> The remains of Maurice Higgins were buried on the 19th from the residence of his mother at Missoula. The parade was one of the largest ever seen in that city, and the body was followed to the grave by many sorrowing friends. During the service banks and business offices were closed. The Missoula Volunteer Fire department, of which deceased was a member, acted as pall-bearers.
>
> *The Columbian,
> August 25, 1892.*

The key witness, Paul Goldenbogen (still recovering from his gunshot wound and extremely weak) was brought in on a stretcher and placed within inches of the jury, so his "labored and painfully spoken words" could be heard.

He, as well as another witness, identified John Burns as the killer. The defense, however, called it a case of "mistaken identity," asserting the defendant had been on West Front Street at a house of prostitution when the crime occurred. Oddly though, Burns couldn't recall exactly which house of ill repute or any other pertinent details.

When the jury proclaimed Burns guilty of murder, he remained as before, "unmoved ... (without) any expression on his face."

Even at his execution the night of December 16, 1892, "as the sheriff slipped the rope over his head and adjusted it," he looked at Father Guild who stood at his side and at the boys "perched on trees nearby" to watch the event, and smiled. When asked if he had any final words, John Burns replied, "No. Let her go."

> "Jack, is there anything more you want to say?" "No," he replied, "Let her go." There was a rattle, and the murderer shot quickly down to death. There were just two slight heavings of the chest and he hung motionless.
>
> *The Livingston Enterprise,*
> *December 24, 1892.*

This story from more than a century ago is replayed to this day as part of historian Bob Brown's characterization of Christopher P. Higgins, performed at "Stories in Stones" and at other Missoula events.

Chapter 12

TRAIN NO. 58 HIJACKED!
HEADS FOR MISSOULA AT BREAKNECK SPEED

These days, it's hard to imagine hundreds of unemployed Montanans marching down to the local railyard to hijack a freight train as their conveyance to Washington, D.C., to demand the president and Congress create a jobs program.

It's probably even more of a stretch to imagine that a lot of us – even our local elected leaders – would support them, offering up food and supplies for the journey.

But it actually happened more than 100 years ago.

Let's set the scene. It's the early 1890s, the economy has tanked, banks are closed and businesses have failed. There are labor troubles and mine closures. The railroads have over-extended, forcing massive layoffs. Unemployment is running as high as 50% in some areas.

General Jacob S. Coxey. Library of Congress.

Jacob Coxey, an Ohio businessman, called for a march on Washington to demand jobs. Thousands responded. They became known as Coxey's Army, Coxeyites, Commonwealers or Industrials.

In California, Charles T. Kelly started a similar movement, dubbed "Kelly's Army."

Early on, Montanans were generally sympathetic. They handed out food and offered places to stay for the night as the unemployed made their way eastward.

But by the spring of 1894, some of the most militant started forming their own "armies." One was led by William Hogan. Organized in Butte and trained in a "vacant lot east of Meaderville," Hogan's group of Commonwealers grew rapidly – eventually numbering 700.

On the morning of April 19, 1894, they marched to a nearby railyard and surrounded Northern Pacific's No. 60 freight train. They found it wanting, though – too few cars to accommodate their numbers – so they marched back to camp.

62

U.S. marshals began guarding train yards and depots. Despite that, four days later, Hogan's Army commandeered an engine and eight box cars.

They were slowed in the eastward journey by a cave-in at the Bozeman tunnel, allowing 30 federal marshals (in another train) to catch up with them.

The posse attacked the hijackers a number of times. When they reached Livingston, their leader, Marshal McDermott, pulled out of the chase but others continued.

The marshals made their final assault on the Commonwealers at the Billings railyard on April 25. Despite hundreds of spectators standing about, shots were fired, a Coxey leader was fatally wounded and one marshal was badly hurt. Two innocent bystanders were hit by bullets.

The spectators turned on the marshals, joining Coxeyites in disarming them. One reporter called the posse "a gang of legalized assassins."

Upon hearing the news out of Billings, Charles Kelly, the leader of 2,000 Commonwealers in Iowa, proclaimed: "I fear our case is ruined. We are now reduced to the level of a mob. I would give my life to have this day's work undone."

The hijacked train was finally stopped near Forsyth by the Army, which dispatched six companies (300 soldiers) from Fort Keogh. The Commonwealers were put under guard and later taken back to Billings.

The mood was rather quiet in western Montana, by comparison. But it was changing.

The *Missoulian* newspaper, initially somewhat sympathetic to the cause, had now labeled Coxey and his followers "an irresponsible set. It is

THERE'S WAR AT BILLINGS!

Industrial Army and U. S. Marshals Come Together.

ONE KILLED, SEVERAL WOUNDED

Marshals Surrender and Are Now Surrounded by The Mob.

Headline, gun battle at Billings. April 25, 1894.

THEY DO COMPLY WITH THE LAW.

The Montana Coxeyites Surrender to U. S. Troops.

Coxey's surrender in Billings. April 26, 1894.

comprised of men whose brains are weak and whose judgment is poor indeed."

The railroad bosses demanded their conductors stop "allowing" the Commonwealers to board trains.

> "Where are your Marshals? Where is the military? Where's Grover Cleveland? Where the —— is anybody? How in thunder do you expect one poor damn Irishman to stop the whole Coxey army?"
>
> *Newspaper clipping, May 19, 1894.*

That drew a sharp retort from the superintendent of the Montana division to headquarters: "Where are your marshals? Where is the military? Where's Grover Cleveland? Where the ---- is anybody? How in thunder do you expect one poor damn Irishman (conductor) to stop the whole Coxey army?"

In the early morning hours of May 19, a couple hundred Coxeyites appropriated "freight train No. 58, eastbound, at Heron and started for Missoula at breakneck speed," reported Missoula's *Western Democrat* newspaper.

> **COXEY'S BOLD BOYS**
>
> Steal a Train at Heron and Start for Missoula.
>
> Pursued By Deputy United States Marshal Haley and a Posse – Traffic Suspended on This Division – Taken to Helena.
>
> *Headline, Western Democrat, May 20, 1894.*

The train "swished past stations at the rate of 25 to 30 miles per hour," stopping only briefly at Trout Creek for water, said the *Missoulian*.

At the request of the local Northern Pacific superintendent, Sheriff Ramsey put together "a small army of deputies" who boarded a special train in Missoula and headed out to intercept the hijackers. Higher-ups at NP, however, ordered the deputies' train recalled, saying they had turned the case over to the U.S. marshal.

It was early evening by the time the feds and their posse arrived from Helena and headed north from Missoula aboard their own train.

At 5:55 p.m., the *Western Democrat* reported, the marshals confronted the Coxeyites at Arlee, where the hijackers were repairing tracks, "which had been torn up for a considerable distance by order of the superintendent." The mob surrendered "without a struggle."

In the end, a few thousand of the unemployed did reach Washington, D.C. But Jacob Coxey was arrested for trespassing on the lawn of the Capitol and wasn't able to make his speech.

A handful of the Commonwealer organizers in Montana did jail time for stealing trains, but most of those arrested were simply released.

Coxey at the Capitol on May 30, 1914. Photo courtesy Library of Congress.

Twenty years later, on May 30, 1914, "General" Jacob Coxey with an army of eight (rather than the thousands he had expected) finally made his speech on the Capitol steps. By then, there was little or no support for his cause.

Rep. Tom Stout (newspaper editor turned Montana congressman) personally observed the moment, and sent his acerbic observations to the state's newspapers.

"I gazed with greatest admiration upon the footsore followers," he recalled.

Each, he said, had "been confronted by dread terrors in the guise of offers of employment by farmers and others … but they remained true to their colors and their cause."

Chapter 13

THE BON VIVANT BARBER
AND THE DECEITFUL DRESSMAKER
– SCANDAL AND MURDER –

It was a scandalous Montana murder case. With a cast of high-profile characters caught in a web of infidelity and jealousy, it was worthy of a titillating novel.

Ed Hart and his wife Eva arrived in Red Lodge about 1900. Hart, described as a "dashing barber," quickly found employment at a local tonsorial parlor operated by Jack Wilkes. Meantime, Mrs. Hart opened a dressmaking parlor.

But that's not why Red Lodge residents remembered the pair.

What they remembered, vividly, was Mrs. Hart attracting "considerable attention by wearing bloomers and riding through the streets astride her horse ... making frequent public displays of her plump legs and dressing in a manner to attract public attention," wrote the *Red Lodge Picket* newspaper.

That "got herself considerably talked about and on several occasions extracted the jealous wrath of her husband, who frequently upbraided her for her conduct and on one occasion gave her a beautiful black eye."

> horse. By making frequent public displays of her plump legs and dressing in a manner to attract public attention she got herself considerably talked about and on several occasions excited the jealous wrath of her husband, who frequently upbraided her for her conduct and on one occasion gave her a beautiful black eye. The day she left Red Lodge her husband was supposed to be in Helena, but when she reached Billings he surprised her by being at the depot. When she alighted from the train in company with a male companion her husband charged her with infidelity
>
> *Red Lodge Picket,*
> *October 7, 1902*

They also remembered the day, six months after the pair's arrival, that Mrs. Hart left Red Lodge, alone, in disgrace, boarding a train for Billings. At the time, Mr. Hart was said to be in Helena. On arrival in Billings, "she alighted from the train in company with a male companion," only to be confronted by her husband (who promptly accused her of infidelity).

"The next morning, she departed for Butte and got her name in print by occupying a room at a hotel with Mr. Wilkes (Mr. Hart's Red Lodge employer), who had preceded her to that city."

Following the Wilkes affair, she proceeded to reinvent herself as Ruth LaBonta or "Madame Ruth LaBante," operating dressmaking parlors "as a blind." Her rooms were next door – and apparently conveniently connected – to the residence of one James W. Kelley, editor of Butte's *Inter-Mountain* newspaper.

The *Red Lodge Picket* reported, "It is averred that the two were married ... and that the fact was kept secret for reasons best known to the parties to the compact." The assertion, though, was never proved.

Madame Ruth LaBonta, Butte Inter Mountain, December 8, 1902.

Now we arrive at the fateful night of October 11, 1902. As reported by the *Anaconda Standard*, "It appears that Kelley attended a banquet given at the Finley (and) had (been) expected to be out late and the LaBante woman knew that."

Kelley "complained of not feeling well and asked to be excused. He was known to be jealous of the object of his affection, and it is now supposed that he had reason to believe the woman was not faithful.

"At all events, Kelley went to his room shortly afterwards and opened the door (to La Bante's room) by means of his key." There he confronted Dr. Henry A. Cayley (a prominent Butte physician) and fired two shots at him as LaBante stood nearby in her nightdress.

The story became a national sensation. "(D)octors express no hope for Cayley's recovery," the *St. Paul Globe* reported the next day. "Kelley, who is still at large, is believed to be hiding in the city. His capture is thought to be a matter of but a few hours. Dr. Cayley is one of the best-known physicians in the city and is married. Kelley is single."

Kelley turned himself in the next day, while LaBante quietly skipped town – reinventing herself, this time,

EDITOR AT BUTTE SHOOTS A DOCTOR

J. W. Kelly's Revolver May Be the Death of Dr. A. H. Cayley.

Saint Paul Globe, October 13, 1902

BOTH CHARGED WITH MURDER

Editor Kelley and Madame LaBonte Held Responsible.

FOR THE DEATH OF DR. CAYLEY

Kalispell Bee, October 28, 1902

as "Mrs. O'Moore" in San Francisco, changing residences at least three times and eluding capture for six weeks. When arrested, she told police it was she who had done the deed!

Dr. Cayley, she claimed, had been infatuated with her. When she refused to go away with him, a struggle ensued, she grabbed a pistol which "accidentally discharged twice and one of the bullets struck Dr. Cayley." LaBante insisted "J. W. Kelley was at no time present and had nothing to do with the affair."

At her arraignment, she appeared in a heavy black veil, but looked like "a young woman who had not a thought of trouble," according to the *Butte Inter-Mountain*. Men, women and children packed the courtroom to hear her "not guilty" plea.

BUTTE ADVENTURESS DROPS FANCY ALIAS

As She Answers to the Name of Eva Hart When Arraigned for Murder.

HER MERRY LAUGH ROUSES COURT

Butte Inter Mountain, December 8, 1902

Meantime, Kelley claimed it was he who shot Cayley – albeit in self defense — believing the man to be a burglar.

Finally, on April 27, 1903, after a two-week trial, the well-known Butte newspaper editor was found not guilty. He promptly left town to stay with his brother, Robert, in Anaconda.

Kelley's admission in court that he'd shot Dr. Cayley, coupled with having been found not guilty of the crime, eliminated any case prosecutors might have had against Madame LaBonte. Her case was dismissed the next day.

Both of our main characters then literally disappeared from any public mention in the press, with one (and possibly two) exceptions.

In a single sentence in the *Daily Missoulian* six years later, in 1909, James Kelley and his brother Robert of Butte were said to be "in the city on business."

And, there was this, in the *Billings Gazette* in 1908, with a dateline of Omaha: "Sewell Sleuman, reputed to be worth half a million dollars ... tonight shot and killed Eva Hart, whose company he had been keeping for some time and then took his own life."

Could it have been the same Eva Hart? Alas, no. Further research reveals no connection -- Omaha's Eva Hart was not Butte's Eva Hart.

Chapter 14

THE MISSOULA & CEDAR CREEK PIONEER
MISSOULA'S 1ST NEWSPAPER

While there's no official certificate on file, most historians agree the community of Missoula Mills dates to around November,1864. For my purposes, though, the birth was delayed another six years, awaiting one critical component.

By Old West standards, a bonafide town required three things: a livery, a bar and a newspaper. By that reasoning, Missoula became a town on September 15, 1870, the date on which the first edition of the *Missoula and Cedar-Creek Pioneer* appeared.

MISSOULA AND CEDAR-CREEK PIONEER.
Devoted to the Development of the Leading Material and General Interests of Missoula County, Montana Territory, and the Northwest Generally.
VOL. I.]   MISSOULA CITY, MONTANA TERRITORY, THURSDAY, SEPTEMBER 15, 1870.   [NO. 1.

Over the years, the *Pioneer* morphed into the *Missoulian*, although the latter prefers to list 1873 as its origin – the year the newspaper was officially named *"Missoulian."* *

In any event, the Magee brothers' *Missoula and Cedar-Creek Pioneer* made quite a spectacle upon its arrival in town – if its reporting on itself is to be believed.

"The citizens of Missoula, and those on the road between here and Helena, were agreeably surprised a few days since by the sight of a printing office on wheels. The motive power for the locomotion of this welcome freight was twelve mules gaily caparisoned with miniature national flags, etc. The wagons containing the outfit were also embellished with banners and other devices, and bore the name of this paper in letters two feet long, upon every part where the legend could find a place."

So far, I'm willing to buy the story.

But it continued: "(T)he enthusiasm manifested by our citizens baffles adequate description. A score of

LOCAL INTELLIGENCE.

A NOTABLE EVENT. — The citizens of Missoula, and those on the road between here and Helena, were agreeably surprised a few days since by the sight of a printing office on wheels. The motive power for the locomotion of this welcome freight was twelve mules, gaily caparisoned with miniature national flags, etc. The wagons

Missoula and Cedar Creek Pioneer, September 15, 1870.

brass bands would have been a 'Quakers meeting' by contrast with the surging and tumultuous uproar of welcome which greeted the advent of the wagons containing the appliances of 'the art preservative of all arts.'

"At first, the drivers in charge of the teams imagined that our people had made a mistake in their time reckoning, and we're only then celebrating the Fourth of July. Becoming assured of the true state of affairs by the repeated and vociferous 'Hurrah! for the Missoula Pioneer,' they cracked their whips, helped to swell the general din, and trod along with conscious pride in the share they had taken in the pleasing event. Even the animals who had hauled the heavily-laden wagons over the mountains from Helena seem to be elated by the infectious hilarity which surrounded them.

"A general holiday was taken for the remainder of the day, and the groups of our citizens who threw themselves into 'hollow squares' during the evening, for the laudable purpose of discussing the great event and certain bibulatory compounds, testified that the day will long be remembered as a 'red-letter-one' in Missoula's calendar."

At the end of the account, an "Editor's note" enlightened the reader who may have actually believed he had slept through a major event in the city's history without having noticed: "The 'feast of reason and flow of soul' that prevailed on the auspicious occasion above recorded may have somewhat confused our local reporter's ideas while fixing events and his memory for after record."

The remainder of the content in Missoula's first newspaper was, for the most part, unremarkable – a report on the Territory's population, a summary of Montana's "mineral and agricultural resources" and various dispatches from eastern and regional publications.

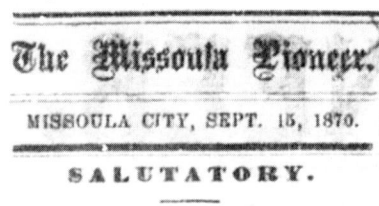

September 15, 1870.

However, its "salutatory" remarks to the "enterprising and energetic citizens of Missoula (the garden county of the Territory)," while perhaps understandable in the social and political context of the times, still takes one's breath away.

The *Pioneer* proudly proclaimed: "For the advancement of all of the varied interests of our beautiful mountain land, and in advocacy of securing all the social and political privileges to its white citizens, we shall labor unceasingly. We shall deal in no gentle mood with those in our midst who would impede the onward march of empire by fostering and giving employment to heathen Asiatic slaves in preference to the free-born, large-souled and intelligent white men who have ever composed the glorious vanguard of American civilization." Bald-faced racism – openly and proudly stated in Missoula's first newspaper.

It would be lovely to say much progress was made over the next three decades, but that wouldn't be the case. On December 2, 1896, the *Ravalli Republican* newspaper in Stevensville printed the following advertisement: "When you go to Missoula, don't patronize cheap Chinese restaurants. And you don't need to go to high-priced hotels either to get a good meal. Try the Rankin House restaurant and you will get a first-class meal for 25 cents, cooked and served by white people."

It presents a disquieting view of life in Missoula as the city approached the 20th century.

###

Chauncey Barbour, a later publisher of the Missoulian, agreed that either date was accurate. "It would be perfectly legitimate at this time," he wrote in 1879, "to claim regular succession in the newspaper line in this county to the 15th of September 1870, and to number our paper the tenth volume," instead of the seventh.

Chapter 15

ENGINE NO. 452 ARRIVES
MISSOULA BECOMES A RAILROAD TOWN

Imagine Missoula County with a population of 500,000. Then imagine that population increase occurring in less than 10 years. For that to happen, there would have to be some incredible event; some unprecedented circumstance. While it's improbable, it's not unprecedented. That kind of growth did actually happen – once – in Missoula history.

In 1870, Missoula had about 2,500 residents. Those first white settlers were drawn here by the fur trade or by gold discoveries in the region. Once here, they also found the land was perfect for agriculture. Still, there wasn't all that much growth. Missoula's population remained at about 2,500 in 1880.

But in the next 10 years, the number soared to 14,427.

What happened? What incredible event occurred? What

Team of eight mules pulling a covered wagon at Fort Benton, Montana. UM Archives & Special Collections.

unprecedented circumstance caused such a boom?

Transportation – specifically, the railroad.

In 1883, the Northern Pacific was close to connecting its eastern and western legs in southern Montana. As it turns out, that connection happened just east of Missoula.

Before the railroad came to Missoula, it was difficult at best to travel to, or bring goods to, the Garden City. Transportation was limited to boat, horse, mule or foot. Missoula relied on huge pack trains from the east, west or south, and then only during fair weather months.

So it was a big deal when the railroad came. In fact, for the better part of a year, area newspapers carried weekly, front-page progress reports of track laying.

By January 1883, the rail line from the west was still 90 miles away, near Weeksville, west of Plains. Still, the Northern Pacific planned to complete that section of the line by summer – amazing, considering the rough, intimidating, virgin terrain.

Artillery, explosives and drills were used to clear rock from mountainsides. Forty carpenters were dispatched in the dead of winter to Marent Gulch (Evaro Hill) to start building a huge trestle spanning nearly 800 feet, at a height of more than 220 feet.

There were similar challenges east of Missoula, including the "Big Blackfoot crossing." In areas between the rivers and gulches, graders were busy preparing for the track layers.

By early June 1883, it was all coming together. The *Weekly Missoulian* noted, "On Tuesday, June 5, 12,200 feet of track were laid. Mr. Winston has promised all his men a new hat if they get to Missoula by the 26th of June."

> Railroad Items.
>
> On Tuesday, June 5, 12,200 feet of track were laid.
> Mr. Winston has promised all of his men a new hat if they get into Missoula by the 26th of June.
>
> *Weekly Missoulian.*
> *June 8, 1883.*

A couple of weeks later, the newspaper's editor rented a carriage, drove out west of town and viewed the progress, remarking, "We caught a glimpse of an engine, and a thrill of pleasure ran over our frame as we thought how many years the coming of that locomotive had been looked for by the old-timers of Missoula."

We'll presume those track layers got their promised new hats, because the first train rolled into Missoula at 4:50 p.m. on Saturday, June 23, 1883, three days ahead of schedule.

There was no shortage of hyperbole in the area press. The *New North-West's* Missoula correspondent proclaimed, "The long agony is

Locomotive in Missoula, circa 1883. Courtesy UM Archives & Special Collections.

over and Missoula is a railroad town." He continued, "Engine No. 452 steamed slowly inside the city limits, and was welcomed by the thunder of cannon, a lavish display of bunting, the cheers of the assembled populace, and last but not least the opening of Frank Worden's celebrated barrel of N.P. whiskey, which has been hidden in Worden & Co.'s cellar for about 20 years."

> *Correspondence New North West.*
> MISSOULA, June 25.—The week just passed has been one of excitement for Missoula. The entire talk has been railroad, and each evening citizens met, compared notes, watched for the headlight, and wagered cigars, hats, etc.. upon the date of its arrival with a perfect looseness.
> ARRIVAL OF THE IRON HORSE.
> But now the long agony is over and Missoula is a railroad town. At 4:30 p. m. on Saturday, engine No. 452 steamed slowly inside the city limits, and was welcomed by the thunder of cannon, a lavish display of bunting, the cheers of the assembled populace, and last but not least the opening of Frank Worden's celebrated barrel of N. P. whiskey, which has been hid in Worden & Co.'s cellar for about twenty years. Those
>
> *The New North-West,*
> *Deer Lodge, June 29, 1883.*

In explanation of that last reference, 14 years earlier (in 1869) Sam Wilkinson of the North Pacific had visited Missoula to discuss the prospects of the railroad coming to Missoula. Over drinks at Worden & Company, Wilkinson, Christopher Higgins and Frank Worden set aside a barrel of whiskey to celebrate the future event, whenever it might occur.

By 1883, though, Wilkinson was 67 years old and too frail to travel. He sent a letter to Worden and Higgins telling them to share the whiskey with the "thirsting crowd," but "when by measure it has sunk to a quarter of the barrel ... pull out the spigot ... then roll the precious and patriotic residue into your cellar as my property." The remaining spirits were sent to Wilkinson in New York (presumably by rail).

Meantime back at the celebration, the track-laying crews were paid and the "red hot" Saturday night drinking began. It lasted well into Sunday morning, when "the cooler was full, and the city authorities were looking for (more) cell accommodations."

The men had only a few days to sober up, before heading out to help on the eastern flank, where progress had been slightly slower. There was concern inside the Little Blackfoot tunnel, where material kept falling from above. Some thought it better to blow "the whole top off and make a big cut of it," but an inspector recommended shoring it up with timbers instead. Meantime, pile drivers still had to finish work at Rattlesnake Creek.

In early July, upwards of 30,000 railroad ties were floated from Warm Springs to the mouth of the Blackfoot to help complete that section of rail.

In August 1883, N.P. officials ordered that all buildings in Missoula, except those owned by the company, be moved back at least 250 feet from the rails. The company had big plans for its permanent depot, encompassing passenger and freight areas, gentlemen's and ladies' rooms, an extensive platform and a second story to house company offices.

At the end of that month, Northern Pacific President Henry Villard, a German-born journalist-turned-entrepreneur who raised millions of dollars from his European connections to take over the line a couple of years earlier, announced plans to gather international dignitaries in New York, then transport them west to Montana in two special trains for the golden spike ceremony. It was to be an exclusive affair – by invitation only – with former U. S. President Ulysses S. Grant joining Villard on the podium.

But when the day arrived (Saturday, September 8, 1883), an estimated 2,500 uninvited Montanans showed up at Gold Creek east of Missoula, ignoring Villard's plans for a private affair with his 400 international guests.

James Mills of the *New Northwest* newspaper reported that Villard "had erected a grand pavilion, and had taken up a quarter-mile of the main track in front of it, that his guests might see it relaid rapidly to the point of union, where the last spike ... should be formally driven."

> **THE NORTHERN PACIFIC FORMALLY COMPLETED.**
>
> That which was in some respects the most memorable and magnificent event that ever occurred in Montana, took place at the Independence crossing of the Northern Pacific railroad on Saturday, September 8th. President Villard assembled there from Europe and the United States some 400 guests, many of them distinguished gentlemen, eminent in the eyes of the world for their learning, character, titles, or money. There were
>
> *The New North-West, Deer Lodge, September, 1883.*

Northern Pacific – Villard Excursion, 1883. Frank Jay Haynes, photographer, Montana Historical Society.

Mills called the event "impressive and picturesque," but also pointed out the "ridiculous (and) spectacular deception" of faking the final spike driving, given the fact trains had been rolling over that spot continuously for a fortnight.

He also noted the arrogance of Villard who through much of the ceremony turned his back on the locals who had not been invited. Ulysses Grant, however, before driving the final spike, acknowledged the crowd and the role of veterans and pioneers who had opened the West to white settlement. The uninvited crowd went wild.

to be favorably impressed. The effect will be to enhance Northern Pacific stocks, secure what further loans it wants and thus put money in the pocket and power in the hands of Henry Villard. On the occasion referred to he was indifferent, even to the discourtesy of turning his back, to the people of Montana, and until the last moment he had never invited but two of them to be present at the ceremony. To the extent that it has been deemed worth while to notice it, this and other indifferences have been the occasion of some indignant expressions toward the President of the Northern Pacific. We

The New North-West, Deer Lodge, September, 1883.

Puck, a national satirical magazine, featured the ceremony on its October cover. It took a jab at Villard, in the form of an unflattering characterization of a "cowboy talking to a British nobleman who is standing on papers labeled 'Brutality, Vulgarity, Insolence, Arrogance, Selfishness, [and] Boorishness,' with an 'Invitation N. Pacific R. R. Opening – Villard' extending from his pocket."

Still, it was the seminal moment for Missoula. The arrival of the railroad allowed this place to grow from a somewhat insignificant Western town to today's modern Garden City.

Perhaps there's a lesson there for those among us who might not appreciate the importance of improved transportation, in the form of modern air travel and timely connections, to Missoula's future potential for growth.

Chapter 16

RAILS EXPAND TO BITTER ROOT

A. B. Hammond produced "some excellent wine and cigars" for his guests – a virtual who's who of western Montana. There were 35 in all including Territorial Governor Preston Leslie, Ex-Governor Samuel T. Huaser, A. M. Holter, E. L. Bonner, Major P. Ronan, Captain C. P. Higgins, W. J. Stephens, R. A. Eddy, F. H. Woody, Henry Beckwith and many more.

A.B. Hammond, Courtesy UM Archives & Special Collections.

They came from Helena, Butte, Bozeman, Deer Lodge and Missoula to board a special train, "made up of a caboose, passenger coach and Supt. F. W. Gilbert's private car" for the inaugural trip – the "first passenger train over the newly constructed railroad up the Bitter Root valley," according to a *Missoulian* reporter who chronicled the extravaganza.

The unnamed reporter, likely the publisher or editor of the paper, gushed about every aspect of the trip and about Hammond, who in later years would be vilified in the press as the "Missoula Octopus," controlling not only the Bitterroot rail line but banking, lumbering and nearly everything of value in the region.

BOOM! BOOM! BOOM!

The Bitter Root Railroad Opened Up In Good Style!

Headline, Missoulian. December 1887.

But on this afternoon in late December 1887, the story was one of progress and growth as the train pulled out of Missoula on the new southern tracks. As they passed over the Bitterroot River bridge near the Buckhouse Ranch, they noted a "good-sized camp of Chinamen, who have been engaged in (road) surfacing work but have gone into winter quarters." While the area was familiar to everyone who'd observed it in the past from the wagon road, the path of the new tracks offered a different perspective on the land.

They made good time between Missoula and Florence, where Hammond showed off H. P. Heacock's timber operation, which was producing lumber for the Butte market. The train slowed considerably as it climbed the grade at "Bass' Hill," where "a goodly portion of the hill had been thrown into the river, and rip-rapping will now have to be done to prevent it from being washed away in high water." At Tyler Station, near Stevensville, a number of additional dignitaries joined the excursion. They included John B. Catlin, Major McCormick and Tyler Worden.

It was late afternoon – nearly dusk – when the train pulled into Hamilton, "the future great county seat and queen of the valley metropolis." In reality, the town was still "in its infancy," where "a good many people were living and doing business in tents." Hammond's guests, however, were lodged at the Grand Central Hotel and the Russ House.

The next day was highlighted by a tour of the Curlew Mine near Victor. On that particular day in 1887, 25 men were laboring underground at the 315-foot level moving tons of ore said to "contain 60 percent of ruby silver." None of the excursion party was allowed to travel down the shaft to view the operation first-hand – as it was "not considered advisable," a reminder of the risk taken daily by Montana miners.

The Curlew visit completed, the party boarded the cars for the trip back to Missoula. At Stevensville, they were not only delighted with a fine lunch, but each member of the party was given a copy of the local paper, the *Northwest Tribune*, literally hot off the press. The newspaper, published slightly earlier than usual in order to be ready as the train pulled into the stop just west of Stevensville, contained an account of the excursion thus far, which delighted the guests.

While the trip was designed to be a celebration of the new rail line, it actually made some news along the way. The *Missoulian* reported that "Governor Hauser, A. B. Hammond, and Chief Engineer Reardon and his assistant, Engineer Govan, in a quiet way practically settled the fate of Corvallis by deciding to continue the road

Governor Samuel T. Hauser, Courtesy UM Mansfield Library – Montana Memory Project.

on the west side of the river to at least as far as the wagon bridge near Skalkaho. Gov. Hauser suggested that the railroad folks give half the amount (toward construction), if the Corvallis people or the county would give the other half."

Business completed, arriving back in Missoula the travelers were wined and dined at "an elegant supper which Mr. Hammond had wired Jones, of the Bon-Ton Restaurant, to have prepared."

With rail lines now connecting both Missoula and the Bitterroot to the rest of the Territory and the country, the population exploded. Missoula grew from a small town to a respectably sized city within the next decade. The Bitterroot expanded as well, justifying its split into a separate county in 1893.

Chapter 17

SNAP & PRINCE
MISSOULA'S FAMOUS FIRE HORSES

With growth came building, but many early buildings were simply fire fodder. A few early business buildings burned to the ground not once, but repeatedly. It soon became clear that fire departments (with fine, athletic fire horses) were a necessity in the towns and cities of the West.

They had names like Mack, Prince, Tyler, Baby, Joe and Snap. They were elite athletes, immortalized in death.

Missoula Fire Station, circa 1897.

The legendary Baby, according to the *Kansas City Journal*, was "one of the best horses the (New York) fire department ever had." As the story goes, when Baby was deemed beyond her useful life, she was told she'd be sent to the auction block, whereupon she drooped her head and died.

In Kansas City, when Joe died of injuries suffered in a June 1894 fire call, Professor E. D. Eames of Kansas State University, a skilled taxidermist, was called upon to make a mount of the veteran fire horse for display in the K. C. fire headquarters.

Missoula had no shortage of famous fire horses. Perhaps the best known were Snap and his brother, Prince.

Snap, the fire horse, and dog, 1894. Courtesy UM Archives & Special Collections.

Snap began his career in 1889, described as "an intelligent animal, standing seventeen hands high, and well trained for his work." Paired with his brother, Prince, they were a perfectly matched team that hauled the fire company's steamer to numerous conflagrations for over a decade.

Prince and Snap "ate smoke at the Hoag House fire in 1890, when the big hotel that stood between the Rankin house and the corner on East Front Street was destroyed."

When the Northern Pacific Hospital burned in 1891, the local press reported the pair "made the famous run, fairly galloping into the hearts of the firemen, and assuring (themselves) of a home in the Missoula fire station" for the rest of their lives.

At times, Prince was said to have "pawed the earth and snorted out his impatience at the inability of the firemen to conquer the flames as quickly as he was wont to see them conquered by the hose he brought for that purpose."

Snap was the first to die, at age 22, in 1901. "He was game up to the last," bounding out of his stall only to fall prone." It was only then that firefighters discovered he was ill. Within a few hours, he died with a "heavy groan."

That marked the beginning of the end for Prince. As A.K. Fox of the fire department told reporters, "It would be useless to attempt to break in a single horse to match Prince."

Prince. Missoula fire horse. Courtesy UM Archives & Special Collections.

Prince died 18 months later, in 1903, at age 24. Fire Department Captain MacAuley "spoke kindly" of his friend at the horse's burial.

A local scribe noted "the lonesome feeling prevalent at the fire station (where) occasionally a fireman will turn and look sorrowfully at the vacant stall, while he mutters, 'Poor old Prince.'"

For years, watching the fire horses practice was one of the great entertainments in Missoula.

"The fire department will make a test run to the depot at 7:30 this evening," declared a local newspaper. "The playful little blacks are expected to paralyze all previous records."

In 1893, "The fire horses were out within ten seconds after the tap of the bell, and within seven minutes hose and hydrant were playing water ten blocks away."

A year later, in another drill, "the two running connections were made with the fire plug at the corner of Higgins Avenue and Front Street (with) water being thrown through one hose in 20 seconds ... and in 23 seconds the next."

> The fire boys gave an excellent drill last evening and made a magnificent display of manouvres. The fire horses were out within ten seconds after the tap of the bell, and within seven minutes hose and hydrant were playing water ten blocks away.
>
> *Missoulian, July 28, 1893*

Fire-horse teams by the early 20th century had become so legendary, officials at the St. Louis World's Fair sent out invitations to "every fire department in the entire country" to send teams to participate in competitions to determine "the best type of fire horses."

Chief May of the Missoula Fire Department received an invitation, but the city wasn't able to accept.

Occasionally, there were shortages of trained fire horses. In Butte, the *Anaconda Standard* loaned its horse, Charley, to the local department in 1895, noting that while the animal had no training for the job, "he is well known as the most intelligent horse in the city and can learn anything with ease."

The fire horse era quickly ended around 1910 when Missoula city officials began to look at "horseless" equipment. The new fire machines promised lower costs upfront, and lower maintenance costs long term.

On June 16, 1911, "the new white speed-wagon" arrived in Missoula. Ironically, it was transported to the fire station ... by a team of horses.

Chapter 18

THE BEE HIVES – BARGAIN STORES OF THE 1800S

Remember the "five & dime" stores? Every town seemed to have one. Inexpensive candy, toys and, well – just about everything, were crammed into aisles so narrow it was best to turn around rather than try to pass another shopper.

By the 1950s and 1960s, many of those independent, locally owned variety stores were replaced by large discount chains – TG&Y, Woolco, Kmart, Shopko and Walmart. Now, of course, it's huge box stores and warehouse outlets.

But did you know the concept of a nationwide chain of large discount stores dates back to the 1800s, with locations from Newark and Chicago to Glendive and Missoula?

The Bee Hive store at Higgins and Main, Missoula, 1894.

They were called "Bee Hive" stores, and the business model was described in Joseph Siryin's book "Carson Pirie Scott: Louis Sullivan and the Chicago Department Store" as "inexpensively acquired inventory sold in high volumes at bargain prices, with its name suggesting the resultant intensity of sales activity within its walls."

Even though everything was discounted every day, store operators still managed to have "specials" and advertised them heavily. Helena's outlet, Genzberger, Barnett & Company, said, "Everything must go ... our prices will be cut to meet the purses of all." And when they said "everything," they meant everything – toys, dolls, wheelbarrows, crockery, lamps, desks.

Missoula's store, called the Chicago Bee Hive, would regularly cut regular prices by a third or more for "five days only!"

CHICAGO BEE HIVE

127 ROLLS OF CARPET AND 250 RUGS AND ART SQUARES AT ONE-FOURTH TO ONE-THIRD OFF OF
REGULAR PRICES

FIVE DAYS ONLY

Saturday, Monday, Tuesday, Wednesday and Thursday.

Bee Hive ad – Missoulian, 1900.

The building at the corner of Main and Higgins, was a "rickety old structure" with a bulging north wall. It was so unsafe, the fire marshal ordered barricades placed on the sidewalks in 1894 in case it took "a notion to tumble down." The owner, a fella named Sablotzsky, apparently was not inclined to make the investment, selling the place to Mrs. Kate McCormick and leaving the repairs to her.

J.J. Stipek's Bee Hive Cash Store in Glendive advertised "women's handbags made by the most reliable makers, at greatly reduced prices," from 75 cents to $10, and "hole-proof hosiery – six pairs guaranteed for six months, $1.50."

A few years ago, when discounters like Walmart expanded to offer grocery items, they were following the Bee Hive model. Fort Benton's Bee Hive sold "Malaga grapes, apples, pears and oysters" along with the "finest imported and domestic cigars." Neihart's store advertised "fine watermelon ... ice cream and fresh Montana strawberries."

Wilson's Bee Hive, at 33 W. Park St. in Butte, didn't limit its advertising to low prices. They ran a promotional contest in 1902 to find the city's "most popular boy or girl under 13 years of age." All you had to do was clip the coupon in the *Butte Inter Mountain* newspaper, fill in the youngster's name and address, and drop it off at the store. Prizes included "a perfect steel range, about one quarter the size of an ordinary range, valued at $15 ... a music box (and a) large handsome doll."

Wilson's Bee Hive ad – The Butte Inter Mountain, 1902.

In a follow-up ad, Winnie Lindusky, 315 Watson Ave., was reported to be leading the "girl" entries by a considerable margin, with 233 votes. Willie Davis, 411 E. Mercury, led Earnest Woodbury, 617 Henry Ave., by 20 votes for the boy's prizes.

The Bee Hive on Central Avenue in Great Falls advertised its "5, 10, 15, 20 and 25 cent counters." Not to be outdone, the Neihart Bee Hive claimed it was "selling goods cheaper than Great Falls."

Many of the Bee Hive stores operated as though they were going out of business – on a regular basis.

"The Bee Hive stock will be sold the next ten days at sweeping discounts," advertised the Kalispell Bee Hive, located on First Avenue East. "Those who have tickets, present them and get the benefit of this slaughter of prices. This stock must all be sold, and we agree to sell this as low as it can be bought at wholesale. Fine chinaware at half price. This gives you an opportunity to save your honest dollars. Everything goes." And you thought that was a modern-day sales ploy!

Bee Hive ad, Kalispell Bee newspaper, 1903.

> Bee Hive Store.
> The Bee Hive stock will be sold the next ten days at sweeping discounts.
> Those who have tickets, present them and get the benefit of this slaughter of prices. This stock must all be sold, and we agree to sell this as low as it can be bought at wholesale.
> Fine chinaware at half price.
> This gives you an opportunity to save your honest dollars.
> Everything goes.
> BEE HIVE STORE.
> First Avenue East.

While most Bee Hive stores began disappearing from the retail landscape by the early 1900s, some lasted for decades more. I wonder if some of today's discount centers (the ones with those price match guarantees) would honor any of my old newspaper ads from the 1800s?

Chapter 19

A BRIDGE, A LEOPARD SKIN & A DEAD END STREET

Few stories have so many divergent elements – the gold rush, the hanging of a road agent, the birth of a famous Missoulian and a leopard skin. They're all connected to – of all things – construction of the Madison Street bridge over the Clark Fork River.

Our story begins in 1872. A Missoula pioneer who became wealthy in the lumber business was awarded a contract to build a bridge. No, not the Madison bridge – the contract was for a Higgins Avenue bridge to connect the downtown with Missoula's growing south side.

Six years later, in 1878, that same bridge-builder-pioneer-lumberman built a house at 134 Madison Street. The home was described as "the showplace of Missoula" – after all, it had the first bathtub in town!

John Rankin home, 134 Madison Street, Missoula. Courtesy UM Archives & Special Collections.

Upstairs, rumor has it, a road agent from the gold rush days was "hanged from the rafters," as the home was being built. While historically unlikely, it's still an interesting story.

The homeowner was John Rankin. He was elected to the Missoula county commission that same year, 1878. His son, Wellington D. Rankin, became Montana's attorney general in 1920.

But it was a daughter, Jeannette Rankin, born in the 13-room home in 1880, who most people remember (the first woman elected to Congress, known for her votes against entering both world wars, namesake of the Jeannette Rankin Peace Center, etc.).

By the mid-20th century, though, the house stood vacant and decaying. One of the last occupants, Mrs. Glenn Berger, said it still contained a room with a leopard skin wall and a painting "with real rocks and moss inside the frame," according to a newspaper story.

Ultimately, the Rankin house and a dozen others were ordered demolished – they stood in the way of progress. The bridge builder's house must make way for another bridge. Post-war America was in a road and bridge building frenzy. President Eisenhower's Interstate Highway System was well underway.

Locally, Missoulians overwhelmingly approved three bond issues in 1956 to build the Madison-Arthur Bridge, a new Higgins Avenue bridge, and the Russell-Lincoln span across the Clark Fork River to replace the old California Street crossing.

John Rankin portrait. Courtesy UM Archives & Special Collections.

Work on the Madison Street bridge commenced in 1957. The concrete work took just over a year. Then work on the approaches began in August, 1958. A massive rock crushing plant was set up behind Dornblaser Field to provide base gravel for the approaches, while other crews put a huge, 15-foot-diameter steel pipe (over 250 feet long) in place to carry irrigation ditch water under the approach.

Meantime, demolition equipment was dispatched to John Rankin's house at 134 Madison. On Tuesday morning, September 30, 1958, "a roaring machine undid the work of the carpenters, stonemasons and other craftsmen who put together the mansard-roofed house," wrote the *Missoulian*.

Bridge construction. Courtesy UM Archives & Special Collections.

Also coming down was the historic McWhirk home, which predated the Rankin house. That home, just south of Front Street, was believed to be the first in town built of brick.

Once the homes were razed, bridge crews could build up the approaches: 90,000 cubic yards of fill was deposited in record time, allowing vehicle traffic across the span by late 1958.

The source of that fill material leads us to (as Paul Harvey would have said) "the rest of the story," involving accusations of hanky-panky between The University of Montana and the City Commission, a restraining order and a highly publicized court battle, a street to nowhere, a lot of mutual back-scratching and the curious tale of Campus Drive.

When you travel to The University of Montana on Sixth Street, then turn right on Maurice Avenue, you'll dead-end just past the Music Building in front of Fine Arts. Maurice Avenue picks up again about four blocks south, at East Beckwith. What's up with that? And what does that have to do with the Madison Street bridge? Patience, my friend.

There was a time when Maurice Avenue was a through street. The story of how that changed leads us to 1956, when U-M was still called M-S-U. University President Carl McFarland requested that the Missoula City Commission close a four-block span of Maurice between Connell and Keith. The university had big plans and needed the space.

McFarland argued the road was "dangerous to students," since it cut through the campus. Besides, he said, it was "worn out." The city agreed, passed a resolution to that effect, and in October of 1956 ordered gravel barricades to close off the campus portion of Maurice Avenue. But Mrs. Edna Bulen would have none of it. She, with her husband as her lawyer, obtained a restraining order, and forced a trial in the spring of 1957.

Bulen argued that Maurice Avenue was purposely allowed to crumble by the inaction of both the University and the City. She charged, "the City Commission would not patch it," and the University had deliberately let the road fall into disrepair, "because McFarland didn't want to pay to have the work done."

She wasn't alone in opposing the street closure. Mrs. George Fox testified it would cut off access to the Women's Club Art Building and Planetarium. There was concern fire trucks would have trouble reaching campus buildings. Others felt their property values would be affected. Former Mayor Ralph L. Starr even reminisced to the court about his days as a street car conductor in the area.

Maurice Avenue as a through street. Aerial photo by Rollin H. McKay, April 30, 1955. Courtesy UM Archives & Special Collections.

President McFarland testified for three hours, outlining the University's multi-million-dollar expansion plan, which he claimed would be jeopardized if that section of Maurice Avenue were not closed. "We'll just have to start it (the plan) over again," he said.

University lawyers asserted M-S-U owned the land on both sides of

Maurice Avenue, extending to the center of the road; thus, the university and the city had the legal authority to close the street. That sparked "a flareup between the lawyers," reported the *Missoulian*. "The University lawyer said if the plaintiff lawyer made it necessary he would go ahead and prove (it), even if it took considerable time. He had eight large deed books, weighing a total of about 100 pounds."

Bulen, meantime, contended that if Maurice Avenue was closed through the campus, residents would be forced "to use an inadequate M-S-U service road on the east edge of the campus to get to the Van Buren Street bridge." What's worse, she said, that service road along the backside of campus at the base of Mount Sentinel was closed during sports events, albeit only a handful of times a year.

Then a couple of curious things happened. First, a local contractor told the court "Maurice Avenue very definitely should be closed," given traffic and safety problems. Second, the University's maintenance engineer testified that M-S-U had "plans for a bypass around the east side of the campus," which would connect with the new Madison Street bridge. But he wouldn't disclose details.

The plaintiff's lawyer found that "intriguing," but all he could get out of the University's maintenance engineer was a hint that M-S-U might have found a way to build the bypass at less expense than repairing Maurice Avenue through campus. Why the mystery? All he would say was, "I'll tell you all about it in a couple of weeks."

After hearing both sides, the court sided with the City and the University. Four blocks of Maurice Avenue were closed, between Connell and Keith. As for all that mystery and intrigue, let's fast forward one year, to late summer 1958.

It was time for that 90,000 cubic yards of fill material to be dumped in place to create the approaches for the new Madison Street bridge. Only then did Missoulians learn that contractors got the fill material from the side of Mount Sentinel, behind campus, in exchange for building a north-south through street to be called Campus Drive, thereby compensating for the closure of Maurice Avenue.

And there you have it – a bit of Missoula history to contemplate each time you drive over the Madison Street bridge to or from campus or Griz football games.

Chapter 20

MISSOULA OFFICIALLY BECOMES A TOWN
HOUSE BILL 105

As mentioned in an earlier chapter, 1883 was the year the Northern Pacific completed its track-laying, making Missoula a railroad town – except for the fact that Missoula wasn't officially a "town."

So, March 1, 1883, House Bill 105 (the act of incorporation) was introduced in the Montana Legislature. But arguments broke out over which Missoulians would be allowed to vote on the matter: property owning tax-payers, or just tax-payers.

Missoula, circa late 1980s. Courtesy UM Archives & Special Collections.

The *Helena Weekly Herald* reported Representative Allen spoke in opposition to the property qualification, telling "a little story of the voter who rode to the polls upon a jackass worth one hundred dollars, the price of a property qualification in Kentucky." A year later, the jackass had died, so he had to walk to the polls. When he "was refused his vote, (he) asked the judge this pertinent question: 'Say, Judge, was it my jackass that voted a year ago or was it me?'"

The Legislature decided the voting rolls would simply be made up of Missoula tax-payers who had been residents for at least six months. The bill was quickly passed and went on to the governor for his signature. The measure created the section east of Pattee street as the first ward, and the area west of Pattee as the second ward. Voting in the first ward would be held at the school-house; the second ward, at the courthouse.

The charter election was held Monday, March 19, 1883, with 63 voters casting ballots for incorporation, five against. Everything happened so fast that Duane J. Armstrong, the *Missoulian* editor, wrote, "The whole charter affair was sprung up so quickly, and the election followed so fast upon its heels, that we had no time to form decided positions either pro or con. And, now that we have got our elephant, what are we going to do with it?"

> —And now that we have got our elephant, what are we going to do with it? An election takes place on the 9th day of April—two weeks from next Monday, when a Mayor, four alderman, city attorney and town clerk, city assessor and town treasurer, one town marshal and one police magistrate are to be elected. After they are installed to office, they must be paid for their work. The
>
> *Weekly Missoulian, March 23, 1883.*

The charter required there be "one mayor, two aldermen for each ward, one police magistrate, one town attorney and ex-officio town treasurer and collector, and one town marshal" – and the election was supposed to happen in two weeks!

A series of local citizens' meetings were held, a ticket was put together, and on Monday, April 9, 1883, Missoula's taxpaying residents overwhelmingly made Frank Woody the newly-incorporated town's first mayor, with a majority vote of 86. Frank Worden, R. A. Eddy, W. C. Murphy and S. T. Arthur were elected to the aldermen slots and H. C. Myers became the city marshal. Almost all the candidates were unopposed.

> OUR CITY ELECTION passed off very quietly, the only contest being for the offices of Marshal and Assessor and Treasurer. Frank H. Woody, Esq., will fill the onerous duties of the Mayor's office for this infant town, while the Aldermanic honors will be supported by Messrs. Frank L. Worden and R. A. Eddy, from the First ward, and Sam I. Arthur and W. C. Murphy, from the Second. A pretty fair Board you will allow. For Police Magistrate, Mr. John L. Sloane received a handsome vote, and offenders against the peace and dignity of the city may rest assured that the usual five dollars and trimmings will be impartially assessed. As City Marshal, Mr. H. C. Myers represents the people's choice.
>
> *Election results, New North-West newspaper, Deer Lodge, April 20, 1883.*

Just ten days later, Thursday, April 19, 1883, the first meeting of Missoula's city council convened in Frank Woody's downtown office. The Missoula reporter for the *New North-West* newspaper in Deer Lodge said, "Our city fathers... concocted a lot of ordinances, bearing on every subject in the Decalogue. The ordinances haven't been posted yet, nor has the marshal filed his bond, so the boys can run the town for a few days according to their own sweet will."

Now it would be reasonable to assume that those very first "concocted ordinances" would reflect the highest priorities facing the newly-minted, officially-incorporated town. If that was the case, it seems the good people of Missoula were tired (literally) of not being able to get a decent night's sleep for all the racket in the Garden City. A noise ordinance was among the first laws passed, and the reviews were swift in coming.

From the *Dillon Tribune*: "The city council of Missoula has dealt a death blow to the brass band of that town by passing an ordinance prohibiting noises at night." From the *New North-West*: "...a fellow now can't even serenade his best girl...without becoming liable to a fine and imprisonment." The new city fathers also passed "a dog law, a hog law, a petty larceny law, and a law to punish vagrants," according to the *Missoulian*.

> The city council of Missoula has dealt a death blow at the brass band of that town by passing an ordinance prohibiting noises at night.
>
> *The Dillon Tribune, May 5, 1883.*

The town's new police officers, Keyes and Nugent (no relation to the contemporary, long-time City Attorney Jim Nugent), went to work straight away gathering up vagrants caught drunk or begging or both. But, where to put them? Aldermen Worden and Eddy approached the county commissioners May 4, 1883, to ask for help. The commissioners agreed to allow a temporary jail to be constructed on the courthouse yard, with the provision that it could be ordered removed at any time by the county.

All of this new law enforcement had a downside. Between the noise ordinance and the vagrancy laws, local saloon-keepers (initially among those who supported raising Missoula "to the dignity of an incorporated town") began "bucking and kicking," according to the *New North-West* newspaper accounts.

Before incorporation a fellow could come to town and "get on a hurrah (and) spend his money freely." Now, "he has to walk easy. One misstep and the Argus-eyed guardians of public peace" toss him in the cooler, fine him, and give him second thoughts about ever coming into town again.

Chapter 21

CITY COUNCIL CIVILITY LOST
"DON'T TALK TO ME THAT WAY, YOU DIRTY LITTLE SCRUB!"

Folks these days routinely complain about incivility in politics and government, but it helps to have a little perspective. Not too many years after Missoula officially incorporated in 1883, rudeness ruled at a some of the council meetings.

The meeting on the evening of October 15, 1890, serves as a good example. The gathering started out routinely enough. The minutes of the last such gathering were approved, routine bills were paid, a petition was received to extend the city's fire jurisdiction south to Second Street, and matters of streets and bridges were discussed.

But that's when normalcy and civility ended and, as a reporter for Missoula's *Weekly Gazette* put it, "The fun began."

Alderman Fussy "moved that the office of street commissioner be abolished ... a polite way of 'firing' Alderman Osborne, who had been appointed to that office a month or so ago."

Osborne shot back that City Attorney Reeves had already determined there was nothing in the statutes to prevent him from holding both offices.

Before anyone could discuss the matter, Alderman Matthus quickly seconded Fussy's motion "and he and Alderman Bennett asked for the roll to be called on the motion."

> **OUR ALDERMEN.**
>
> A Regular Monkey and Parrot Time in the Council.
>
> The Harmony and Brotherly Love in that Body Shown---Osborne Fired.
>
> *Missoula Weekly Gazette, October 15, 1890.*

Osborne interrupted the clerk, who'd begun calling the roll, asking "that other members of the council be given a chance to talk."

Matthus jumped in, asserting it was a "measure of economy (referring) to the Main Street grading." Bennett agreed, saying, "That work was let out at $0.57 a yard, when it might have been let at less figures."

And the gloves were off.

Osborne: "Yes, the trouble is that you did not get the work yourself."

Matthus: "I didn't have the lowest bid."

Osborne: "You had a bid for 40 cents."

Matthus: "No, I did not."

Osborne: "You had a man of yours put in a bid for you in his name."

Matthus: "There was a bid in at 40 cents a yard."

Osborne: "Yes, and what kind of bid was it?"

Matthus: "I guess the bid was all right."

Osborne: "I'll just prove it right now that that bid was one which no one could legally accept."

Finally, Mayor Kennedy interrupted; the discussion was getting too personal.

But the volleys continued.

Osborne said the whole attempt to abolish the office of street commissioner "was all a piece of spite work because certain parties did not get the contract."

Fussy: "We want to abolish it as a matter of economy."

Osborne: "Where does the economy come in? You cannot get along without a street commissioner.".

Fussy: "We'll show you when we get through with this."

Donley: "I move we adjourn."

Aldermen Gussy and Bennett: "There is a motion before the house. The motion to adjourn is out of order."

Donley: "A motion to adjourn is always in order."

Fussy: "Not when there is a motion before the house."

City Attorney Reeves: "A motion to adjourn is in order at any time."

Fussy: "What have you got to do with this? You are not running this council, I want you to understand. The people of Missoula elected us to run the affairs of the city."

Reeves: "Yes, and the people of Missoula elected me to see that you do it right."

Fussy: "Well, you just keep your mouth shut."

Reeves: "Don't talk to me that way, you dirty little scrub!"

Fussy: "I'll talk as I please."

City Attorney Reeves—Yes; and the people of Missoula elected me to see that you do it right.

Alderman Fussy—Well, you just keep your mouth shut.

City Attorney Reeves—Don't talk that way to me, you dirty little scrub!

Alderman Fussy—I'll talk as I please.

City Attorney Reeves—You daren't talk that way to me after we get out of the council chamber, you little pinhead. If you do I'll mash your face!

Loud cries for order and vigorous pounding on the mayor's desk made the two subside.

Missoula Weekly Gazette,
October 15, 1890.

Reeves: "You daren't talk that way to me after we get out of the council chamber, you little pinhead. If you do, I'll mash your face!"

Mayor Kennedy had had enough, pounding his gavel, demanding order, and reminding the assembly he was in charge "by God!" and did not propose to have aldermen run things.

"This sudden wakening up of his honor," reported the *Missoula Weekly Gazette,* "paralyzed the council, and quiet supreme at once reigned."

A vote was called on abolishing the office of street commissioner, and it passed 6-1, with Osborne, inexplicably, among the "ayes" – only Donley voted "no."

Finally, a motion to adjourn was made. But it faltered on a 4-3 vote "and another heated discussion began," with Alderman Bennett suggesting the office of police chief be merged with the duties of street commissioner.

At that, Aldermen Angevine, Donley and Osborne simply got up and left, leaving the rest with no option but to adjourn.

The *Gazette* summed up the whole affair rather succinctly: "So ended one of the finest exhibitions the city council has yet given the people who elected them."

The next time you find yourself dismayed at the lack of civility in modern times, just close your eyes, think back to 1890 and sigh.

Chapter 22

PENMANSHIP, HYGIENE & BOYS OF RAWHIDABLE AGE
– MISSOULA'S 5ᵀᴴ ANNUAL TEACHERS' INSTITUTE –

October 1887 was wet in Montana – rainy and muddy. Eggs were scarce, too. Among the weather and commodity reports in the local papers were some brief items about education.

On the opening day of school, Miss Van Fleet (one of three teachers at Missoula's schoolhouse) found a box on her desk. Inside were a piece of rawhide and a note.

"Miss Van Fleet," said the note, "I think you will have use for this."

The local newspaper, while acknowledging that "some of her boys are of rawhidable age," assured readers "Miss Van (Fleet) will govern her scholars with love, and the boys are indeed tough who can withstand her winning ways."

A couple of weeks after school commenced, the rawhidable-aged boys had a three-day reprieve, as Missoula hosted the area's fifth annual Teachers' Institute.

For many participants, the mere act of attending that conference took considerable effort. You didn't just carpool for a short drive from Hamilton or Plains. Remember, it was 1887. Miss Louise Schaplay had to leave Thompson Falls on Saturday to attend the Monday-through-Wednesday events.

J. R. Faulds, the editor and publisher of Stevensville's *North West Tribune*, hosted the conference, which opened

> MONDAY.
> Organization of the Institute.
> What we are here for—J. R. Faulds.
> Reading and Writing (Primary)—Mrs. S. O. Murray.
> Number Work—Miss Ethel Galloway.
> Language Lessons—Miss Buck.
> First Lessons in Geography—J. L. Duffy.
> Vocal Music in the Common Schools—Miss Tillie Rosebaum.
> Orthography—Miss Menard.
> Physiology and Hygeine—Miss Van Vleet.
>
> TUESDAY.
> Arithmetic (Intermediate)—Mrs. Tribby.
> Geography—Miss Wal's.
> Penmanship—Mrs. Sue Jones.
> Programme for a Country School—J. J. Boud.
> Civil Government—F. Thomas.
> Voice Culture—R. V. Rork.
> School Government—J. R. Faulds.
>
> TUESDAY EVENING.
> Compulsory Education—W. M. Bickford.
> The Law of Life—R. V. Rork.
>
> WEDNESDAY.
> Grammar—J. J. Bond.
> Diacritical Marking—Miss Shappla.
> Physical Geography—R. W. Miller.
> The Hobby Rider—Miss M.E. Longstaff.
> How to Teach U.S. History—J.W. Tiedt.
> Arithmetic (Advanced)—F. Thomas.
> School Management—R. V. Rork.
>
> WEDNESDAY EVENING.
> Physiology and Hygiene—Dr. F.S. Hedger.
> School officers, trustees and county superintendents; A. C. Logan, territorial superintendent.
> A cordial invitation to attend all the sessions is extended to the general public.
> The evening sessions will be held at the M. E. church.

Teachers' Institute program schedule. Weekly Missoulian, October 7, 1887.

with a round of "Gospel Hymns ... followed by prayer," then the roll call, with "each member respond(ing) with a quotation."

Presentations followed on "Number Work," "Language Lessons," "Orthography" and Miss Van Fleet's discussion of "Physiology and Hygiene."

Hygiene was a big deal in the late 1880s. Typhoid, scarlet fever and diphtheria were commonplace. The *Weekly Missoulian* newspaper ran an account of one man who blamed his illness on a debris pile being used as fill material at Higgins Avenue and Front Street. "It will be remembered that the stench was frightful and was susceptible of being cut with a knife."

Mrs. Sue Jones captivated the assembled teachers with her views on "Penmanship." Today, of course, penmanship (or cursive writing) is viewed as old fashioned and unnecessary – after all, we "keyboard" rather than write.

Miss Tillie Rosebaum had a segment on "Vocal Music in the Common Schools" followed by R. V. Rork's explanation of "Voice Culture." That one sent me to the dictionary.

"Voice culture" is training your "vocal organs" to become more "melodious," by understanding anatomy, psychology and other factors – then training a lot.

Professor Rork "illustrated his ideas on voice culture by a few experiments in which he was aided by Mr. Miller and Miss Buck."

Miss Shappia conducted a session on "Diacritical Marking" (those little marks or signs placed atop letters to help with pronunciation – like "piña colada").

But a presentation by Miss M.E. Longstaff caused a double-take. Her subject was "The Hobby Rider." The ... what?

It turns out "Hobby Rider" was a short story about an annoying richling, written by a fellow with the unusual name of Jerome K. Jerome.

Jerome was English – a playwright, novelist and at times a schoolteacher

Sketch of Jerome K. Jerome. Los Angeles Herald, November 12, 1905.

and journalist – who was best-known for his humor, described by the *Encyclopedia Britannica* as " warm, unsatirical and unintellectual."

Quite by accident, I ran across a book by Jerome a few years ago titled *"The Idle Thoughts of an Idle Fellow,"* published in 1886. The book is still available at a few libraries, or can be found online in its entirety.

I found it delightful. Among Jerome's observations:

• "Idling always has been my strong point. I take no credit to myself in the matter – it is a gift. Few possess it. There are plenty of lazy people and plenty of slow-coaches, but a genuine idler is a rarity."

• "I like work: It fascinates me. I can sit and look at it for hours."

Then, there was Jerome's observation on honesty: "It is always the best policy to speak the truth – unless, of course, you are an exceptionally good liar."

But I've digressed; back to the Teachers' Institute.

There was a bit of unrest. A number of teachers who were scheduled to make presentations didn't show up, requiring attendees to cover for them.

That resulted in a group resolution, "That it is the sense of this institute that those teachers who have unnecessarily absented themselves should receive a personal censure from the county superintendent."

On a more upbeat note, it wasn't all work. After each session, there was a 10-minute break during which the teachers socialized with each other and visited with parents and students who came to observe. Other times, the teachers were entertained by the musically inclined attendees.

These days, MEA-MFT conferences tend to have presentations like "Preparing Youth For The New World of Automation" or my specialty: "Undisciplined Writing." But now, as in the past, teachers had best show up. Remember 1887's resolution to hand out "a personal censure from the county superintendent!"

Chapter 23

MONTANA'S NEW UNIVERSITY
1ˢᵗ GRADUATING CLASS OF TWO

It was Wednesday, June 8, 1898, the day of Missoula's very first commencement at the University of Montana. Montana Governor Robert Burns Smith, members of the State Board of Education, Chief Justice Pemberton and other dignitaries from Helena joined UM President Oscar J. Craig and the university faculty for the ceremonies, held at Union Hall.

Missoulian, June 1898.

Now let's pause for some perspective. So far in our story, everything sounds quite routine and normal. But you have to appreciate how we arrived at this day in 1898. Missoula had been designated the site for the state university in 1893, but funding wasn't approved until two years later.

When classes began on September 5, 1895, the university consisted of a single, eight-room building with only two rooms actually renovated and ready to use. A mere 135 students had registered for classes, and according to one account, "to keep the rest of the state from knowing (of the) small attendance, the first catalogue issued by the institution listed any and everybody connected with the school ... special students, preparatory students and music students." The bit of deception was an attempt to win over well-to-do Montanans who, at the time, were inclined to send "their progeny to eastern schools or military schools." The entire faculty at UM consisted of President Craig and four others.

So, as we return to our story of that lovely spring day in Missoula, it will come as a bit less of a shock for you to learn that the graduating class of 1898 numbered – two: Miss Eloise Knowles (bachelor of philosophy) and Mrs. Ella Robb Glenny (bachelor of arts).

Miss Knowles came from one of Missoula's most prominent families; her father was federal Judge Hiram Knowles. She later went on to the University of Chicago, where she obtained a higher level degree in philosophy, then returned to UM as an Art Department instructor.

Knowles also "founded Theta Pi which became Kappa Alpha Theta in 1909 ... (working) at the university until 1915 when ill health forced her to go to California on a leave of absence. She died on April 9, 1916." Knowles Hall, on campus, is named for Eloise.

Ella Robb Glenny was married to William Mount Glenny, the chief dispatcher for the Northern Pacific railroad in Missoula, a prominent position in town. "They had one child, William Robb Glenny," according to historical documents. The couple later moved to Minneapolis.

Eloise Knowles, one of two graduates. UM Archives & Special Collections.

The graduating class may have been small, but "(t)he hall was packed with friends and acquaintances of the graduating class," wrote the *Daily Missoulian*. Mrs. Glenny's oration, "Some Tendencies in Education," was "worthy of great thinkers" according to the press. Miss Knowles' presentation on "The Expression of Thought" was said to be "well handled and faultlessly delivered." Governor Smith congratulated the pair, then "congratulated the people of Missoula for the great honor that is conferred upon them by having an institution that was capable of turning out such perfect scholars."

William Mount Glenny and Ella Robb Glenny. UM Archives & Special Collections.

Following commencement, a parade formed at Higgins and Main, led by a "cordon of police" and the fire department. Then came the Odd Fellows, Foresters, Elks, Knights of Pythias, state and local officials. The parade marched down Higgins, across the bridge to south Fifth, then east to Maurice and onto the university grounds led by Grand Marshal John L. Sloan, the local police magistrate. At 2:30 p.m. "the laying of the cornerstone of the university (commenced) under the direction of the university building commission." Gov. Smith, acting as president of the state board of education addressed the crowd, and University President Craig summed up the state of "State Education."

More than 50 years later, a member of the founding faculty, Dr. Frederick Scheuch, praised the first two graduates of the university, saying they "brought strength of character, self-reliance and love of beauty" to the campus. His remarks came at the groundbreaking for the new Women's Center in 1952.

Of course much has changed on campus since those first classes were held in the fall of 1895 and the first commencement took place in the spring of 1898. Recent graduating classes at U-M have swelled to over 2,000. Hopefully each one of them benefit as much from their campus experience as Eloise and Ella, class of '98.

Chapter 24

THE JANITOR & THE FOOTBALL TEAM
THE BEGINNING OF THE GRIZ

C.C. "Chick" White was in the thick of it as the players scuffled for the pigskin in a scrimmage at the southside athletic grounds in Missoula. The newly assembled university football team showed promise that October afternoon in 1897, even though many of them had never actually seen a football game and were still learning the rules.

University Main Hall and football field, circa 1900. Courtesy UM Archives & Special Collections.

The weather was raw, so "Chick" opted to keep his coat on over his football uniform. As he and others dove for the ball, he felt "a sharp pain in his left groin," but figured he'd just landed on a small stone in the field.

As he got up, though, he noticed his shoe was filling with blood. He quickly pulled off the uniform and his clothes. He'd been seriously cut. Other players helped apply a tourniquet, then rushed him to Doc Fitzgerald's place to have the wound dressed.

C.C. White wasn't a member of the team – he was the university's janitor. He and others in town had either volunteered or were lured into putting on uniforms to make up a practice team so the university squad would have enough players to scrimmage.

White, as it turned out, was assisting Professor Elrod with some taxidermy work earlier in the day and had forgotten to remove the leather case in his jacket containing knives.

One of the blades – a particularly sharp one – had popped out of the case, carving a 2-inch-long, 1-inch-deep gash in his groin. Another knife sliced his chest.

Neither wound was life-threatening. But, should "Chick" ever return to the practice field, he'd likely remember not to carry any cutlery.

Meantime, coach Fred Smith (a former football player at Cornell and UM's new chemistry professor/chair) continued to prepare the squad for its pioneering season on the gridiron.

There had been a number of attempts at organizing a football program since the university opened. An athletic association had been formed in the fall of 1895 and a quickly assembled team had scheduled its first game for the afternoon of October 19, 1895.

Morton J. Elrod. UM Archives & Special Collections.

The opposing team, the Missoula Giants, was made up of well-known locals with names like Higgins, McCormick and Worden. There were predictions that the game to be held at the city baseball park would spark the football spirit in Missoula and draw a large crowd.

But no press account can be found of the game actually taking place. Later in the year, there were similar reports of more games scheduled, then canceled, so perhaps that's what happened with the first game.

The next year, 1896, the university assembled another squad and scheduled a Thanksgiving Day game with the Garden City Commercial College team, followed by a New Year's Day game in Deer Lodge.

This time, there was press coverage (at least of the second game), but it was not especially charitable to the visiting squad. Of the January 1, 1897, meeting, the Deer Lodge *New North-West* newspaper wrote:

"If the young men composing the Missoula team came here with the notion concealed in their bosoms of pulverizing the earth at the expense of the anatomy of some of our most vigorous young men, disappointment must have set in in the early stages of the game, for it soon became apparent to the spectators that the Missoula team was no match for 'our kids.' "

Deer Lodge shut out UM 18-0 in sloppy conditions on a muddy field.

The *New North-West* did praise the University 11 as a "clever team (that) tried hard," and sympathized with them over their poor treatment at the hands of the "hard-hearted newspaper men of the Garden City."

They quoted the *Missoulian* as saying the loss "was a genuine surprise to those who have watched the Missoula boys practice. They were surprised because the score wasn't about 144 to less than half of nothing."

The Missoula correspondent for the *Anaconda Standard* described the returning UM team as "weary, wet and draggled (with) not much to say about the game with the boys of the Athens of Montana."

By the time the fall season arrived, the university team under head coach Smith was somewhat more prepared for its six-game schedule. The first three games, all against the Missoula Athletic Club Tigers, ended in scoreless ties and two of the final three games ended in losses to the Butte Business College.

The single win of the 1897 season was the November 25th game against the Agricultural College team from Bozeman.

This very first in a long history of intrastate battles was played on a snow-covered field in Missoula, with fans stamping their feet at the sidelines as much to keep warm as to cheer the team.

It was a rough contest. A Bozeman player named Patterson injured his jaw, "but it was put in place" so he could continue playing.

Others from both sides "received wrenches and contusions, but not serious enough to cause them to leave the field. Reno Sayles had a broken finger." And all that was early in the first half!

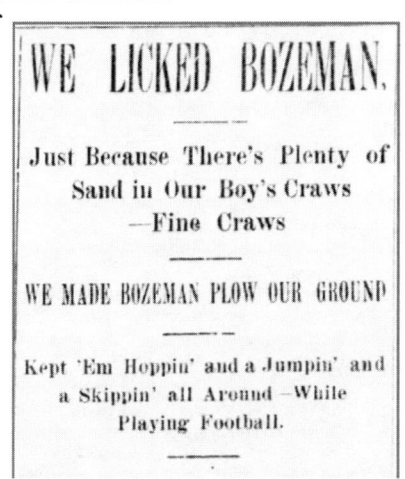

Newspaper headline, 1897.

Extensive local press coverage was lacking as "the *Missoulian's* regular football reporter was unable to be present," and the paper figured since just "about everyone in the town who enjoys the game saw it," there was no need for further detail.

Each year as the Grizzlies begin their season practices, we should all remember those valiant volunteers of the past, particularly C.C. "Chick" White, the brave janitor, for helping our very first UM football players prepare for the 1897 season and their first-ever win against their cross-state rival.

To learn more about UM football history, check out the *"Red Book"* of handwritten notes by legendary coach George P. "Jiggs" Dahlberg, which has been digitized by the University of Montana's Mansfield Library Archives and Special Collections.

> In the meantime, the University team played 3 games against "The Tigers", composed largely of Missoula boys. All 3 games were scoreless ties. The first game against "The Tigers" was reported in The Missoulian of Oct. 23, 1897, by the society editor. The game attracted so much local interest, in fact, that the Missoulian of Oct. 30th, a column and a half was devoted to an explanation of the football rules.

Hand-written note by George P. "Jiggs" Dahlberg.

Chapter 25

TALKING FROM THE SIDELINES COSTS GRIZ THE GAME

*The outlook wasn't brilliant for the Mighty Griz that day;
the score stood 14-12, with but seconds left to play.*

With apologies to Ernest Thayer, author of 1888's "Casey at the Bat," and to all of you for purloining baseball poetry for a football story, the mood was similar on that fall afternoon in 1929 when Griz fans realized their team was moments away from its first loss to the Bobcats in more than 20 years.

The game was played in Butte. The Cats scored early with a kickoff return to midfield, followed by a long pass to an open receiver in the end zone. The score: 7-0.

BOBCATS TAKE GRIZZLIES AFTER TWENTY LONG YEARS

Three Thousand Enthusiastic Fans Whoop Her Up For Winners—Bruins Could Not Produce At Right Time

*Big Timber Pioneer,
October 31, 1929*

It only took five minutes, though, for the Griz to respond, recovering a Cat fumble, then executing four running plays – the final one, a 15-yard scramble for a touchdown. Then they muffed the extra point. The score: 7-6.

In the second quarter, the Grizzlies quickly marched down the field, threatening to score, but fumbled. The turnover, combined with a strange penalty a few minutes later, set up the Cat's second touchdown. Now it was 14-6.

The Griz responded, "(carrying) the ball up the field from the kickoff after the touchdown to make their second score," reported legendary *Missoulian* sports editor Ray Rocene. But again, they couldn't convert the point after, and now trailed the Cats 14-12.

Still, Griz fans weren't worried. There was plenty of time and their team easily maneuvered down the field for what appeared to be certain scores.

Three times in the second half the Griz were inside the Cat's 10-yard line. But they couldn't put it across.

Missoula, in one last effort, marched all the way from their own 19 to the Cat's 5-yard line as the clock wound down, but couldn't run one final play before the gun sounded. The Cat's won: 14-12.

As with many close games, the loss could be traced back farther than those failed, final drives. Twice the Griz misfired on point-after attempts. Then there was that strange penalty early in the game when the Griz led 12-7.

> 20. A Grizzly player on the sidelines was caught talking to his mates on the field and a 15-yard penalty result-
>
> *Big Timber Pioneer,*
> *October 31, 1929*

It was a 15-yarder for "talking from the sidelines" by a player who was warming up. That put the ball on UM's 3-yard line, ending with a Bobcat score.

"Talking from the sidelines?" Say what? Never heard of it. So I turned to some experts. Mick Holien, a longtime fellow broadcaster and "Voice of the Griz," was as perplexed as I. "Talking on the sideline?" No idea.

Next up, Gary Hughes, a colleague of mine in the Missoula Senior Forum, a retired UM associate athletic director of internal affairs and longtime Grizzly Athletics ticket manager. Again, no help – as confused as I.

So I speed-dialed another longtime fellow broadcaster, Bill Schwanke (aka "Grizzly Bill'), and – pay dirt!

Schwanke surmised it must have been "taunting or disruptive vocalizing at the snap." Sounds plausible, and offers a cautionary note for future Griz-Cat games: Shhhhhhh – Quiet on the sidelines! It could cost either side the win.

Chapter 26

THE SMART SET – CIVILITY, CULTURE, SOCIAL ORDER

"Society news" used to be a big deal, even in the smallest of newspapers.

Growing up in Libby in the 1940s and '50s, I can recall the local newspaper, the *Western News*, dialing up our house ... wait, I made a bit of a mistake there. They didn't "dial." They just picked up the phone and asked the operator to be "connected to" our number. Libby didn't get dial phones until late into the '50s, if memory serves. We didn't get TV until much later than the rest of the world, too (this is where you utter a sympathetic sigh).

Where was I? Oh yes, they called to ask my mother about a recent visit of my aunt from the Billings area. The following week, the item was in the paper.

At the turn of the 20th century, society columns were ubiquitous in American newspapers. Many Sunday editions contained large society sections, outweighing even the sports news. The papers covered social events from engagements and weddings, to minutes of social and religious groups, to card parties and out-of-town visitors.

Society news columns can be traced back to James Gordon Bennett Jr., who created one of the first in the *New York Herald* in 1835 dealing with the antics of the well-to-do in society. Although largely satirical, it seemed to catch on with both the general readership and the well-to-do, who apparently liked reading about their own, sometimes tasteless behavior.

> Mrs. Turney's Circulating Library Party.
> Mrs. E. L. Bonner's Reception.
> A very pleasant entertainment was given by Mrs. W. W. Turney at her residence in Deer Lodge last Saturday afternoon, a forecast of which was given in last Saturday's paper. It was the first entertainment of the kind to be produced in this city. Each lady present represented the title of some book, either in dress, action, or something worn on her person, and the lady guessing correctly the largest number of books represented was to receive the first prize. The

The New North-West, November 25, 1893.

In Montana's earliest newspapers, social news and other brief reports were buried under a heading of "local jottings." You might have read about Marcus Daly's visit to town right next to a sentence or two about the arrest of local vagrants.

But in the late 1800s, as Montana became home to more and more wealthy individuals, a number of newspapermen started to emulate their Eastern brethren. The *Helena Independent*, in 1889, dedicated a full column to "The Social World," in which it reported on the "numerous entertainments for society people."

Declaring the gowns worn by local belles to be unusually elegant, the columnist remarked, "Helena has been quite conspicuous among the cities of its size in the West for the tasteful dressing, both for the street and for evenings, of its ladies."

Western Democrat, Missoula, 1893.

Not to be outdone, papers like Missoula's *Western Democrat* greatly increased their coverage of the movers and shakers of society in the early 1890s. They dubbed them the "Smart Set," the "Upper Crust" or the "Missoula 400," and the stories weren't buried – they were on the front page.

Even today, locals can recognize many of the names of Missoula's social elite from 19th century social news in the *Western Democrat*.

"Mr. and Mrs. Beckwith charmingly entertained a select party of friends at their palatial home last Friday evening," read one such column. "Whist was the game furnished for the entertainment of the guests. A sumptuous repast was also served during the evening."

The economy may have been going to hell in a handbasket for most Americans (the crash of 1893), but it remained a gilded age and the 1-percenters carried on.

The *Western Democrat* often reported on a local group called the "Biodas." On one occasion, the group of young ladies "held a 'poverty party' at the residence of Miss Worden on East Pine street. ... The members were attired in the choicest patterns and loudest shades of spring calicoes. Some of the patterns were so loud that they took a hand in the conversation in a mezzo-soprano tone of voice. Some of the latter are 'horrid' enough to insist that the feeling was mutual on this score. Be that as it may, the Biodas claim to have spent a most enjoyable evening."

Bioda's Poverty Party.

The "terpsichorean art" (dancing) was the foundation of many 19th century social events. So, naturally, there were numerous dancing academies to be found in the Garden City and, of course, to run an academy one had to be a "professor."

Professor Holtbuer advertised his "first-class dancing academy at the Realty Hall, where he is prepared to teach the latest styles in the terpsichorean art. Open afternoon and evening."

Meantime, Professor R.D. Owen announced he had "just received the music for the new and latest dances in vogue in the East. The repertoire consists of the Bon Ton, Rivulet, Victoria and Harvard Gavotte."

But that didn't mean all the young men of Missoula's "Smart Set" used their fine terpsichorean skills.

In January 1894, the *Western Democrat* lamented: "Missoula society bewails a scarcity of dancing men. Some of the fairest flowers of the social conservatory are now regularly blossoming along the wall. The men ... are content to pose at the doorways or loll in the smoking room.

"The girls wish in vain for a return of the days of their grandmothers when there were two or more aspirants for the honor of every dance with every girl; when men attached as much importance and took as great pride in the art terpsichorean as women; when the motto of every social gathering was 'On with the dance! Let joy be unconfined.'"

Dance card. Western Democrat, 1893.

Even when local dances were well attended and enjoyed, the newspaper critic could still find fault: "At one of the social dances held in the city recently, there were present a number of ladies belonging to the upper crust of Missoula's '400' who danced nearly, if not quite, the entire program through without removing their hats. There has been considerable criticism indulged in by a number of those who witnessed this affair.

"One gentleman ventured to say it would be in equally as good taste for him to dance with overcoat and overshoes; that if they felt they were any too good to go and remove their hats they should certainly stay away."

Chapter 27

THE BIODA CLUB & LADIES KAZOO ORCHESTRA

It was "a brilliant social event" and "one of the most important of the season," according to the society writer for the *Western Democrat* newspaper. Miss Alice Reeves was to be introduced to Missoula society.

It was the gilded age – 1893. Members of the "upper crust" of Missoula were determined to show that their fine city had the social graces, the savior-faire of their eastern kin.

"The handsome Reeves residence in South Missoula was thrown open for the first time, and this fact, together with interest attending the debut, was the signal for a large attendance. The arriving guests were ushered into a scene where music, flowers and handsome toilets were elements of a beautiful whole."

The guest list included names still recognizable today – Knowles, Beckwith, Bonner, Catlin, Connell, Evans, Higgins, Worden and Keith among many others. "The fair debutante was charmingly gowned," reported the *Western Democrat* and was assisted in welcoming guests by "a number of pretty young ladies."

```
The cast of characters in Monday
evening's entertainment is as follows:
Tableau..........................Pipe of Peace
          LITTLE PAUL P.
Paul Pryor.........................Lenita Bonner
Wilmot Eyre.....................Jimmie Straughn
Tom Fyfe..........................Venie Hoblitzell
Nan Fyfe..........................Carolyn Worden
Bettie Pringle....................Sadie Catlin
Juliette Smythe..................Belle Catlin
          MY TURN NEXT.
Taraxicum Twitters..............Kittie Catlin
Tim Bolers........................Hilda Knowles
Tom Trop..........................Eloise Knowles
Farmer Wheateker...............Helen Hathaway
Cecily.............................Gertrude Hathaway
Peggy.............................Almeda West
          THE COMPANY'S HUSBANDS.
Mrs. Tom Dale...................Frances Robinson
Mrs. Bob Forrester..............Maud Brimson
Miss Dale........................Anna Beckwith
Mysterious Female..............Lenita Bonner
Mysterious Female..............Gertrude Hathaway
                    Orchestra.
```

Cast of characters. Western Democrat, December 1893.

As was common in the 19th and early 20th century, the entertainment included a "delightful repast" of "sweet morsels and all the delicacies of the season" followed by music and dancing to a late hour. Also common was opening the affair with a game of Whist. The card game was all the rage at the turn of the century. It involved exacting rules governing not only how the game was to be played but also to the etiquette of players.

Books were written on the subject – the most likely one used in this period, one written under the nom de plume, "Cavendish." The "head prize" winners that Friday evening in Missoula were Dr. G. P. Mills

Bioda Club phot, circa 1893. Courtesy UM Archives & Special Collections.

and Miss West. The "boobies went to C. Humphrey Hall and Miss Nita Bonner."

Also noted in this particular society column were the secretive "parlor theatricals in rehearsal by the Bioda club." The Bioda club, a young-women's group formed in the fall of 1893, was described by a society writer for the *Anaconda Standard* as being "composed of the wealth, beauty and talent of the Garden City."

One of the first "entertainments" given by the club was staged at "the palatial Bonner residence in South Missoula in December of '93. The society "editress" of Missoula's *Western Democrat* was invited to observe in order to ensure maximum, front-page news coverage.

The "editress" did not disappoint, characterizing the evening as "one of the swellest events of the season," to which only "ladies prominently identified with Garden City social circles" were invited. "The club presented two charming comedies," about which the columnist gushed, "the bevy of society girls...acquitted themselves creditably (and) the splendid manner in which each character was handled, demonstrated a most careful selection as to the adaptability of the artiste."

The following night, the Biodas broke from tradition and invited a few prominent young men to a repeat performance at the Florence Hotel. "The music was furnished by the Ladies Kazoo orchestra under the direction of Miss Fannie Robinson, who wielded a huge cheese knife as a baton," wrote the correspondent for the *Anaconda Standard*.

> room of the Bonner residence. The arrangemens for the entertainment were complete and the affair passed off without a hitch. The music was furnished by the Ladies Kazoo orchestra under the direction of Miss Fannie Robinson, who wielded a huge cheese knife as a baton.
>
> *Anaconda Standard,*
> *December 17, 1893.*

The only hitch in the performance came during a campfire scene involving a peace pipe. The young ladies were not familiar with "the art of smoking," and one of them "became visibly affected, necessitating a rapid descent of the curtain." Nonetheless, the *Standard* writer complimented the performers hoping they would offer more such fare, but added they "should be more generous with (their) invitations."

> The first anniversary of the Bioda club was celebrated in a fitting and most elaborate manner at the Bonner residence, in South Missoula Monday evening. The Bioda club is composed of the wealth, beauty and talent of the Garden City and that Monday night's event would prove to be one of the swellest of the season was a foregone conclusion. The "bal poudre" is a fashionable mode of entertainmnt
>
> *Anaconda Standard,*
> *October 28, 1894.*

The club continued for some years, with references in western Montana journals as late as 1902, but then disappeared from society columns.

What a time it must have been. It's hard to get that image out of your mind – Fannie Robinson with a long cheese knife leading the kazoo band.

Chapter 28

MAN: IN HIS PROPER PLACE
A COLUMNIST NAMED "GLITTER"

Early Montana newspaper society columns soon gave way to local columnists, many using pen names to disguise their true identity. "Glitter," one example, seemed to have little use for men: "I wish to say something to the members of my sex who are unmarried. It is this: Don't get married – that is, if you have an ambition, a purpose in life."

Glitter's column appeared in the *Missoula Weekly Gazette* in the early 1890s. Was the columnist a man or a woman? For that matter, was Glitter truly a columnist, or perhaps the editor of the paper having a bit of fun? We don't know.

For the purposes of our story, we'll assign Glitter the mantle of a woman and (given the headline of this particular column) we'll also assume the writer

> **GLITTER'S GOSSIP.**
>
> Her Advice to Girls Who Want to Marry—Don't,
>
> The Blessings of Celibacy on the Kreutzer Sonata Plan for the Gentler Sex.

Missoula Weelkly Gazette, 1891.

was having a bit of fun, adapting the theme of Leo Tolstoy's controversial novella, "The Kreutzer Sonata," into a local advice column.

Tolstoy's work was published in 1889, the local newspaper column just three years later in early 1892. The questions raised – of love, marriage, sexual abstinence and equal rights – remain as topical today as then.

"If your only desire is to settle down, have a home of your own, and a husband thrown in … this article is not addressed to you. Marry the first good-looking fellow who asks you, and be happy. We are done with you."

Glitter had no time for the "darner of socks," the woman "content to be somebody's darling and nothing more," the woman willing to bask solely in her "husband's greatness," hoping it might envelop her.

No – Glitter wanted to reach "the girls who have ambition, who feel a desire to excel in something, whether it be music or civil engineering."

For those girls, she exhorted, "there must be no marrying … at least until you have tried for yourselves and seen what is in the big world and how much of it is for you. And to do this is not hard. It is simply a matter of concentration, and need not necessitate giving up the smallest pleasure.

> A MATTER OF CONCENTRATION, and need not necessitate giving up the smallest pleasure. Dance, flirt, walk, talk, ride, skate—do everything in fact to enjoy yourself, only at the same time keep always trying to perfect yourself in whatever you think you have talent for. Perhaps not only one, but two or three things. If so, all the better. The cultivation of the one talent may result in the development and perfection of the other two. Bu never lose sight of the goal. Keep that always in view and don't give a darn who says against it.
>
> *Missoula Weekly Gazette, February 4, 1891.*

"Dance, flirt, walk, talk, ride, skate – do everything in fact to enjoy yourself, only at the same time keep always trying to perfect yourself and whatever you think you have talent for. Perhaps not only one, but two or three things. If so, all the better."

But again, she reminded, "Never lose sight of the goal (and) don't get married. "If you do, there's an end of it all. When you allow your interests and aims in life to be coupled with those of some fascinating piece of masculinity then the mischief is done, so beware of handsome eyes and lovely mustaches."

There would be plenty of time for all that later, she said, and "there will be even more and better (men and opportunities) ... if you wait a while."

For now, she advised, make use of these "lords of creation ... in your efforts toward gaining name and fame."

Take advantage of "their susceptibility, their vanity – and it is vast – their tender-hardheartedness, their little weaknesses, make them stepping stones to greatness, levers to push yourself forward, battering rams to break down the barriers which they themselves have raised in your path.

"Show them, show everyone, that you have a determination and they will respect you for it and help you, and be the first to applaud you when your battle is won.

"Not one atom of womanly sweetness or virtue need be lost. Nay, you will gain a thousand-fold more in the contact with the world. Be somebody! Don't be commonplace!"

Of course, following this advice would require the young ladies of the 1890s to be brave.

"Don't be afraid of what people may say about you. Look the world square in the face, and with fearless hand and undaunted heart wrest your laurels from it.

"Fear the world and it will censure you, or worse still, treat you with coldness and indifference; face it boldly, despise its power, and with what slavishness it will fawn upon you, with what eagerness will its tributes be laid at your feet." Signed: Glitter.

In a prophetic column, dated October 29, 1890, Glitter envisioned a day when the reign of men would end – even in politics. "It will not be long before the hand that rocks the cradle and rules the world will also be the hand that rules the polls." In fact, Glitter predicted, "The year 2000 will witness the complete supremacy of woman over man. He in his turn will be the inferior being."

Glitter concluded, "Then man will take his proper place at home, washing dishes, darning socks, tending babies, etc., and then the saying will have to be contradicted for 'the hand that rocks the cradle' will not be 'the hand that rules the world.' The hand that wields the sceptre will be the ruling hand, and will have something better to do than rocking cradles."

GLITTER'S GOSSIP.

When Base Man Will Have to Retire From Power.

Missoula Weekly Gazette, October 29, 1890.

The Glitter columns were short-lived, running periodically between summer 1890 and spring 1891, then disappearing from the Weekly Gazette.

By 1894, a competing paper, the *Missoulian*, having seen all that the *Gazette* and *Western Democrat* had done over the years, decided to publish a tongue-in-cheek society column on their front page. It was hilarious – until its roots were exposed and it abruptly disappeared.

Chapter 29

VIOLETTE GLEAMER – SCANDALOUS NON DE PLUME COLUMNIST

"(An) estimable young lady of this city ... will attempt every Saturday to dish up society as she finds it in Missoula, writing of it in her own particular manner."

With that, the *Missoulian* launched a new society column which would grace the pages of its Saturday editions. The young columnist, the newspaper reported, would write under the nom de plume of "Violette Gleamer."

It was early 1894 and the columns were a satirical jab at the crosstown *Western Democrat's* stuffy social columns on the city's "swell set." While it was widely believed the author was the *Missoulian's* city editor, he issued repeated denials.

It started out innocently enough, with the *Missoulian* and the *Western Democrat* exchanging friendly barbs over the anonymous column, but after a few weeks the series suddenly disappeared amid controversy. But let's not get ahead of ourselves. First, we have to appreciate and delight in these articles.

JANUARY 13, 1894.

THE UPPER CRUST.

Vivacious Violette on Society As She Finds It.

IS THERE A SOCIAL FEUD HERE?

The First Racy Letter From the Missoulian's New Society Correspondent.

Missoulian, January 13, 1894.

The initial "racy letter" by Violette Gleamer appeared on the front page of the *Missoulian* on January 13, 1894, suggesting (oh, my!) that "harmony does not dwell among the entire swell set."

Apropos of factionalism, it was just the other day that I noticed how absurdly silly one of the factions—or rather members of one faction—endeavored to add another of the numberless small absurdities each faction has indulged in to satisfy its desire to demonstrate that the members of this faction—say we call it the South Side Club—do not care to mingle with—well the North Side Club or any person patronizing any of the latter club's members. It

Missoulian, January 13, 1894.

The columnist admonished "the members of perhaps the two leading families of the town (for allowing) anything to intervene to create factionalism. This can but bring about the most undesirable result."

Ms. Gleamer accused Missoula's south-siders of refusing to mingle with

120

the north-siders, citing a recent snub. "One of the masculine leaders in our social set is nothing if not an admirer of one of the prominent members of the North Side Club and for this and for no other reason was he not asked to the reception given by the South Side Club."

The columnist reminded those involved: "During the coming season there will be a number of small parties, composed of members of the swell sets of Anaconda, Butte and Deer Lodge, visiting us, and it would really be a matter of sincere regret if the factionalism which now exists is not done away with."

The following week, under the headline, "VIVACIOUS VIOLETTE VICIOUSLY VIOLENT," Gleamer wrote that she "was somewhat amazed at the very considerable adverse comment (from the swell set) that was passed upon my last article."

"I cannot conceive why they should become offended; what I said was certainly intended for the social betterment of the community, and while the shoe may pinch the feet of the principals in this unfortunate existence of affairs, it will be only temporary."

Violette also found "no little amusement ... by the number of ridiculous conjectures as to the author of these weekly articles; and while I know

> **WE UNS OF THE SET**
> Vivacious Violette Becomes Viciously Violent.
>
> WHOM THE MYSTERIOUS SCRIBE?
> Does She (?) Wear Pants or Pantalettes, is Now the All Absorbing Question.
>
> *Missoulian front page, January 20, 1894.*

of no serious reason why my readers shouldn't know whom I am, I believe that my aims in ascertaining what information I may have to impart will be better served by not just yet publishing my real name."

Over the next few weeks, Violette took aim at the shortcomings of some of the men of the "upper crust." She accused them of poor breeding in everything from eating pie with a knife to parting their hair in the middle, something that "smacks too much of effeminacy, and what is there that disgusts a girl sooner with a man than effeminacy? Nothing, certainly."

Men's collars were "ill-shapen" and no one, in Violette's opinion, could

> **GLEAMER'S GUSH.**
> Vitriolic Violette Not So Viciously Violent Today.
>
> A FEW POINTED SUGGESTIONS
>
> The Usual Week's Dish-Up On the Sayings and Doings of the Local Four Hundred.
>
> *Missoulian, January 27, 1894.*

"tie a four-in-hand scarf well." Their boots were "neglected," their hats "dilapidated," and their nails "shocking (and) deplorable!"

Violette castigated any man who, in his haste to make money, neglected his appearance. The columnist said such dishevelment may be acceptable in business, but not "when he goes out in society. That is an unpardonable breach, and such a man is unbearable."

The article brought a quick rejoinder in the form of a letter to the editor signed, "One of the Under-dressed."

"My dear old maid, girl or mother, which ever you are ... (this) is an age of reason, money-making and horse sense and we poor devils of men have something else to think of besides making parlor ornaments of ourselves for the benefit of the well-bred orbs of our lady friends. It is you women who keep us 'broke' most of the time, it takes money you know to keep you 'smartly gowned.'

"You know yourself, dear Vi, that if Miss So and So went to Mrs. So and So's afternoon tea, or yellow coffee 'smartly gowned' and you were not smartly gowned but just becomingly dressed, you know ... you would go home, stamp your pretty foot, or perchance your No. 7 hoof, and vow you 'wouldn't go again, so there now!' Now honest, wouldn't you, Vi'? That seems to be the general way of your sex, at least."

Ouch!

Meantime, someone signing his name only as "Biodaous," wrote a letter to the editor of the competing newspaper, the *Western Democrat*, to proclaim, "Violette Gleamer is a man ... and it does seem a little strange to me that he should regret the fact that there are no well-groomed men in Missoula." Implying Violette was actually the *Missoulian's* city editor, the writer proclaimed, "Mr. Gleamer was not so well groomed himself the first time I saw him. In fact he looked as if he had not been groomed, or curried either, for some time. He had on a pair of ice cream pantaloons, the bosom of which had refused to accompany him any further in his travels."

The *Missoulian* fired back, "vouching

Biodaous' letter to the editor, WesternDemocrat, February 4, 1894.

its professional honor, in support of the statement that no member of its staff, or any individual connected with this office in any capacity is identified in any manner with the preparation of the articles. The papers, as heretofore stated, originate from an estimable person who stands high in Missoula's society and who is in position to discuss the sayings and doings of their members in manner stated."

Violette, for her part, responded directly to Biodaous, but rather less directly to his charge: "The absurdity of his assertion is so apparent that I shall not attempt to discuss it. Why should people stop to consider whether I wear pants or pantalettes? (Only) a woman — and one belonging to my set, at that — is in a position to acquire the knowledge of our doings and reporting the same weekly to the dear readers of the *Missoulian*. Let us have no more of this mysterious business."

Well, there was certainly more mystery to come.

After a run of only a few weeks, the Violette Gleamer columns ceased as suddenly as they had burst upon Missoula's social scene.

The disappearance coincided with a story in the *Western Democrat* newspaper charging Ms. Gleamer (who it called a "backwoods critic" and "journalistic gypsy" who never had "an original idea") with "gleaming" an entire section of one of her columns from a copyrighted article from the Bacheller & Johnson syndicate. To support the plagiarism charge, the paper printed the two articles side by side.

> In the customary amount of "rot" that appeared in the columns of the esteemed Missoulian a week ago, under the signature of this "Violet Gleamer," the author took occasion at the commencement to apologize as follows: "I refer the reader to every newspaper of prominence in the United States as an excuse for this column. Similar work will be found in all the publications." Alas! This is too true. For the similarity is so marked that we reproduce a paragraph from Violet's gleamings and one from a copyrighted article by the Bacheller & Johnson syndicate.
>
> *Westerm Democrat,*
> *March 4, 1894.*

The *Missoulian* editor responded the next day: "The *Western Democrat* persists in attributing to the Missoulian what it pleases to term the sins and omissions of Violette Gleamer, leaving the inference that this paper is responsible for ... the articles. (We have) assured in every possible manner that the Gleamer papers do not originate in this office, and while, on their first appearance, the authorship was attributed in jest to the city editor of this paper, we do not believe that any of our readers will now believe that to be fact."

The paper went on to quote Violette Gleamer as saying she had "acquired the pernicious habit (plagiarism) from one of her newspaper friends," an apparent reference to a *Western Democrat* editor. The *Missoulian* article concluded its jab at the *Western Democrat* with,

"Take a tumble, Dave, before Joblotzsky's Bee Hive (a local teetering business building) falls down on you."

> The public pardons mistakes. But it hates journalistic malice and newspaper billingsgate. The likes or dislikes of a writer are of little concern to the public. Let him keep them to himself. But when a cow-county critic like "Violet Gleamer" pleads for the reader's acceptance of a column of stolen filth, it is placing a mighty low estimate upon the intelligence of the people of Missoula.

Western Democrat says it was no mistake.

> Violette Gleamer departed this morning for Washington where she will report, exclusively for the MISSOULIAN, the sensational Pollard-Breckenridge - seduction-breach-of-promise- $50,000 - damage - suit, the preliminaries of which appear in the telegraphic columns of this issue.

Missoulian, March 8, 1894.

In the end, the *Missoulian* opted to write the columnist out of the paper, by sending "Vivacious Violette" to Washington D.C. to, "report (on) the sensational Pollard-Breckenridge-seduction-breach-of-promise-$50,000-damage-suit."

While I would never condone plagiarism, I'll admit to a bit of sadness at the demise of the Gleamer columns. They were a hoot at a time Missoulians needed a good chuckle.

Chapter 30

PROPER ETIQUETTE
NEVER PASS PLATE MORE THAN SIX TIMES

At times these days, it seems we all could use a refresher course in civility, manners and etiquette.

Normally, looking to the past offers us some guidance – but, in this case, perhaps not.

Cecil B. Hartley wrote a book on the subject in 1860 titled, *"The Gentlemen's Book of Etiquette, and Manual of Politeness,"* based on "the best French, English, and American authorities."

In it, he wrote, "Man was not intended to live like a bear or a hermit, apart from others of his own nature," and laid out some basic tenets of civility and manners for polite society.

THE
GENTLEMEN'S BOOK OF ETIQUETTE,
AND
MANUAL OF POLITENESS;
BEING
A COMPLETE GUIDE FOR A GENTLEMAN'S CONDUCT IN ALL HIS RELATIONS TOWARDS SOCIETY.

Then, fourteen years later, the editor of a Missoula newspaper suggested a few variations on those social rules and guidelines – variations befitting small Western towns.

First, Hartley's view: "You may set it down as a rule that as you treat the world, so the world will treat you."

He recommended that a gentleman should "carry into the circles of society a refined, polished manner, and an amiable desire to please, and it will meet you with smiling grace, and lead you forward pleasantly along the flowery paths…"

Otherwise, should you "go, on the contrary, with a brusque, rude manner…you will find society armed to meet you, showing only sharp corners and thorny places for your blundering footsteps to stumble against.

"You must meet rudeness from others by perfect politeness and polish of manner."

As for one's manners at the dining table, Hartley observed, "…there is no occasion upon which the gentleman, and the low-bred, vulgar man are more strongly contrasted, than when at the table."

Warren R. Turk, the editor of the *Missoulian* newspaper in 1874, agreed, observing that "half the world appears boorish and uncouth to the other half simply because people are not taught manners."

So, wrote Turk, "We have carefully prepared a few general hints on etiquette applicable to both children and adults, and if anyone is benefited by them, our labor will be amply repaid."

Missoulian, 1874.

Turk then proceeded to set a slightly lower standard than Hartley for early-day inhabitants of Montana.

"Never pass your plate for mashed potato more than six times, especially if there is company at the table.

"Never wipe the back of your neck with your napkin, no matter how hot the day is.

"Don't use your finger to stir your coffee. The handle of your knife is more fashionable, and if you want to be real aristocratic, take a spoon.

"Refrain from wiping your mouth on the table-cloth...your coat-sleeve is much more handy."

On the subject of the proper protocol for calling upon a lady, both Hartley and Turk had much to say.

Hartley wrote, "A call may be made upon ladies in the morning or afternoon; but in this country, where almost every man has some business to occupy his day, the evening is the best time for paying calls."

However, he cautioned, "Never make a call upon a lady before eleven o'clock in the morning, or after nine in the evening."

The *Missoulian's* Turk agreed...I think: "An evening call on a young lady should never be made in the forenoon."

Further, Turk advised, the proper gentleman should closely observe the circumstances and react accordingly.

"If the old man comes in with a shot-gun," he warned, "the call shouldn't be prolonged over an hour."

Hartley, on the other hand, cautioned, "If you see the master of the house take letters or a paper from his pocket, look at the clock, have an absent air, beat time with his fingers or hands, or in any other way show weariness or ennui, you may safely conclude that it is time for you to leave, though you may not have been five minutes in the house."

Turk agreed that a self-sacrificing approach was best. "If you are one of a party making an evening visit, and fruits and nuts are passed around," he admonished, "don't fill your pockets until someone has had a chance. One must be self-sacrificing about such things."

Hartley also addressed tact, tyrannical viewpoints, passion, and anger.

"A gentleman will never use his tongue to rail and brawl against any one; to speak evil of others in their absence; to exaggerate any of his statements.

"Maintain, in every word, a strict regard for perfect truth. Do not think of one falsity as harmless, another as slight, a third as unintended. Cast them all aside."

Thankfully, Turk did not articulate his views on these subjects.

As mentioned at the outset, these thoughts from long ago are offered up in the belief that civility, manners and etiquette could use a re-boot these days, and that – normally – much can be learned from the past.

However, it is probably best to follow Hartley's advice – not, Turk's.

Chapter 31

HELENA'S BROADWATER HOTEL
LUXURY AND COMFORT FOR THE ELITE

The soup was puree of cauliflower, followed by boiled salmon with hollandaise. Entree choices ranged from "Spring Chicken, Saute a la Creole (to) Catelette de veal, aux fine herbes."

The first 150 guests were seated for dinner at 6 o'clock as hundreds more waited. "The dining room force (was) composed of colored waiters, who went expertly about their task, attired in full dress suits."

It was August 28, 1889. Colonel Charles Arthur Broadwater's magnificent new hotel/hot springs resort was officially opened in Helena.

Colonel Charles A. Broadwater – studio portrait by W. H. Taylor of an original likely by F. Jay Haynes – Courtesy, Montana Historical Society

Broadwater, whose social and political circle included Marcus Daly, William A. Clark, and Samuel T. Hauser, had made his fortune in railroads, real estate, and banking.

The Colonel's massive new building, termed one of the largest construction projects in the Northwest, was comprised of "a three story frame on the cottage plan with sweeping porticos on the south front...(and a) mammoth plunge bath."

The *Helena Weekly Herald* reported construction was completed in a single year with timber "imported from Oregon and Minnesota." It was said to have cost a half million dollars.

"All the luxuries and comforts of a nineteenth century hostelry can be enjoyed with as much pleasure as the noted public resorts of metropolitan centres," wrote the paper.

As many as five hundred people flocked to the "brilliantly lighted" hotel via the local motor line or by private carriage.

The Capital City Band played as the guests gathered on the

Broadwater Hotel and Natatorium, Helena – circa 1910.

expansive hotel balconies before touring the corridors "admiring its manifold beauties, reveling in delightful contemplation of lovely etchings and engravings, and enjoying the luxurious surroundings of corridors and apartments."

Each room was "furnished with elegant carpets, Turkish rags and tapestries, hard wood furnishings and furniture of polished mahogany, oak, cherry, walnut and other fine woods.

"After viewing these interior beauties and the brilliant light of myriads of incandescent lamps, not forgetting to pay a visit to the bathrooms, where porcelain tubs that cost over $200 apiece and soft rugs invite oriental luxury, the guests assembled in the office rotunda, where an impromptu meeting was held."

Helena Mayor Fuller told the crowd, "We have found it a splendid structure, commodious in its arrangements and complete and elegant in its appointments, lacking nothing to secure the comfort or gratify the tastes of its guests.

"The bath, with its vast proportions and sumptuous equipment, is calculated to make cleanliness a temptation as well as a duty next after godliness."

"The guests included the most prominent people of Helena. Among those present were all the members of the City Council and their families, besides several hundred of the Board of Trade with their wives and children."

Many of the guests came with bathing suits in hand, but were disappointed.

A FINE HOTEL.

Broadwater's Big Caravansary Thrown Open to the Public Yesterday.

Thousands Visit the Beautiful Building and Admire it in Detail.

Members of the Council and Board of Trade Formally Dedicate it to the Public.

Helena Daily Independent, August 27, 1889.

Broadwater Brochure – Dining Room – UM Archives & Special Collections.

The *Helena Daily Independent* reported, "Last Friday water was turned into the immense plunge bath and by yesterday morning it was full of clear, sparkling water at just such a temperature as would have pleased bathers.

"Unfortunately it was discovered... water was leaking out and the bath was emptied. It was discovered that the immense pressure of water had forced the asphalt bottom loose in several places and it will take some days before the repairs can be finished."

The pool was enormous – similar to the 400 by 200 footprint of the hotel.

The hotel grounds covered forty acres with "clumps of willows and cotton woods being utilized for beauty spots...broken up with patches for the flower beds and fountains which make the place really attractive.

"Winding paths have been laid out, with rustic seats at intervals, making it a model lovers' Paradise, and when the moon fails to shed its beams, electric lights are so stationed that the darkest bowers will have sufficient light to keep footpads from plying their trade."

The bar was said to be "fitted up in superb style" as was the billiard room. Each room was "furnished with hot and cold water...private bath rooms for ladies and gentlemen. Beside the tubs are douche, spray and shower baths. The dressing rooms adjoining are furnished with standing wash stands and careful attendants are always at hand to supply every want."

In addition to the sleeping rooms there was a "big observation tower, which will be a favorite place for visitation. The verandas, which extend the entire front and along both ends, are eighteen feet in width and form a continuous promenade for a quarter of a mile. The veranda is lit with incandescent lamps and plentifully supplied with easy chairs and settees."

By the next year, Colonel Broadwater installed an electric rail system to take guests directly from the train depot to the hotel/natatorium in twenty minutes.

The Broadwater was marketed as the perfect stopover for elite travelers between Yellowstone and Glacier national parks. But, the Colonel had badly overestimated just how many "elite travelers" could be drawn to this opulent retreat in the mountains of Montana.

The project faltered, then began to die with Broadwater's death in 1892. A 1935 earthquake damaged the Natatorium forcing its closure. The hotel permanently closed six years later. Finally, in 1974 the remaining contents of the derelict building were auctioned off and the hotel demolished.

> **THE NEW ELECTRIC ROAD**
>
> How Travelers Will Be Carried to the Beautiful Broadwater By Electricity.
>
> There Will be Neither Dust, Cinders Nor Smoke to Annoy People.
>
> *Helena Independent,*
> *April 29, 1890*

In the following years some of the hot springs were opened to the public and racquetball courts were added.

Today "Broadwater Hot Springs" offers a variety of pools, and a taproom and grill where the table tops are made from "up-cycled 1978 vintage wood floors from the (racquetball) courts."

Instead of the "Spring Chicken, Saute a la Creole (and) Catelette de veal, aux fine herbes" of the nineteenth century, today's fare includes "Big Sky Nachos, the Broadwater Burger, the Wilder Caesar Salad (named for the Colonel's daughter)" and a wine list including Kings Ridge Pinot Gris.

Bon Appétit!

Chapter 32

RAG TIME & TANGO
INTOLERABLE, IMMORAL DANCES

It's perverting souls, and has to be stopped!

Good Catholic parents were warned to protect their children or be guilty before God of failure in their most scared duty.

It was denounced as a keystone in the the overwhelming immorality of the new paganism.

So, what was this threat to goodness, morality and virtue, in the early 20th century?

It was "rag dancing," and more specifically the newest dance craze from Argentina called the "tango." Its impact was immediate and worldwide – touching even small Montana towns.

> **"BOSTON" IS BARRED BY STUDENTS**
> NO MORE RAGGING OR NEAR-RAGGING AT UNIVERSITY DANCES.
>
> *Headline – Missoulian. October 4, 1912.*

> **COMMERCIAL CLUB FERNINST RAGGING**
> Will Give Dance, But Bars Latest Styles In Terpsichorean Art
>
> The Columbia Falls Commercial club went on record as being against "ragging," when the question was submitted to a vote of its members at the regular monthly meeting held Monday evening.
>
> *The Columbian, Columbia Falls, January 22, 1914.*

The etymology and origins of the tango are blurry – perhaps the name is African, the dance Uruguayan or Argentinian. Whatever the case, it was controversial. That's because forms of the dance were popularized in low-class areas, and snubbed by society.

Cardinal Pompili, representing Pope Pius, ordered the tango banished in Rome. The Archbishop of Paris followed suit.

In Albany, New York, Bishop T. M. A. Burke went even further, saying, "I trust that no Catholic in the diocese of Albany will take part in any such dance as the tango, bunny hug, turkey trot or grizzly bear."

The *New York Tribune* reported the ban immediately cost Catholic Charities an estimated $25,000 when they were forced to cancel the Emerald Ball, an annual fundraiser.

New York suffragists, however, successfully used the tango to get men to sign pledges backing their cause. The *Sun* reported, "By merely signing a little slip of paper (from) a vision in yellow and white he will be entitled to dance with one of the ten prettiest suffragists in town. No signature, no dance."

TANGO BAN HALTS CATHOLICS' DANCES

Charity Functions Abandoned at Estimated Loss of $25,000 to Beneficiaries.

New York Tribune, January 18, 1914.

In Montana, reporters asked Bishop J. P. Carroll for his take on the tango. He said he hadn't actually seen it, "but he had heard it had a tendency toward immorality, and therefore the church would be opposed to it, as it was to all things possessing similar tendencies."

Within a few weeks, though, a Paris newspaper reported the Pope had removed the ban after viewing "a princely Roman couple perform the dance for him. He was quoted as saying, "Persons of your age must dance. But why adopt the ridiculous and barbarious contortions?"

Students attending the February, 1914, Helena high school senior ball loved the "Boston" and the "Tango" – but, not their principal. A. J. Roberts abruptly halted the dance, when one of those intolerable, "immoral dances" was attempted. The students revolted – walked out – and took the dance to the Placer Hotel ball room.

Meantime, in Missoula, dance instructors were promoting the tango, and the local Bijou Theater booked "Barton and Balle, tango dancers extraordinary" who would perform "all the latest dances."

TANGO CASUS BELLI IN HIGH SCHOOL UPRISING

HELENA STUDENTS REVOLT AGAINST ORDER PUTTING NEW DANCES UNDER BAN.

"Casus Belli" (event justifying war) ends high school dance, Missoulian, February 13, 1914.

Missoula stores began selling tango shoes, tango beads and tango hats.

The local paper ran an extensive story in its Sunday society section in February, 1914, announcing that, "Missoula has at last yielded... finally won (over) by the seductive...Tango Tea."

According to the *Missoulian*, "Private (dance) classes have increased in membership amazingly during the last few weeks," with "lately-won enthusiasts" offering, in their defense, that the tango "abounds in terms of art."

The society writer minimized the controversy over the "suggestive and immoral" new moves, allowing that the criticism was "perhaps justified" initially, but only because of poor execution of the dance. New forms of the tango are now "stately and graceful."

In fact, the local critic went as far as to say, "...in no figure of the tango is it correct for the gentleman to come in closer proximity to his partner than three or four inches. Hugging may be permissible at times and places, but it forms no part of the tango gracefully and rightly danced."

By March, 1914, the tango had enveloped our nation's capitol and, it seemed, even Montana's "Seat B" Representative Tom Stout.

Tom Stout. Courtesy Montana Memory Project, UM Archives & Special Collections.

Splashed on its front page, the *Missoulian* reported, "Tom Stout is taking tango lessons – sly as he has endeavored to keep it. Accused of it, the Montana representative indignantly denies it – but blushes when he says it."

Indeed, capitol reporters had discovered that 'ol Tom had been making regular trips to a local theater at odd hours. They confronted the resident dance instructor, who delightedly described the talents of his new charge.

The article speculated that when Rep. Stout returned to his home state in the fall, "...if anybody hopes to put it over on Tom with the sagebrush slide, the grease wood glide or the Treasure state trot, they'll have to go some."

Soon enough, though, the new terpsichorean expressions became widely accepted, as would be their successors – Charleston, Rock n' Roll, Disco, Hip Hop – each, with its accompanying dose of controversy.

Perhaps our musical history is trying to teach us – in the words of Sheryl Crow – that we should just lighten up, and, perhaps, "have a little fun before (we) die." But, we should probably stop short of "a good beer buzz, early in the morning."

Chapter 33

HIJINKS OF THE ROYAL AND UNIVERSAL ORDER OF MYSTIC HIJIS

Hiji is the name of a town of less than 30,000 people on the southernmost Japanese island of Kyushu. It's the home of Harmonyland Theme Park. Hiji is also the name of an elbow blow in the art of Karate. None of this is of any particular help in explaining why the name "Hiji" was given to members of a fun-seeking secret society formed in Missoula early in the 1890s.

The group was officially named "Monarch Moslem, No. 196, Sons of the Mystic Tie," and was created on April 5, 1891, as an "association of gentlemen banded for the diffusion of benevolence, charity and good will to all."

Although the genesis of the group is elusive, it was likely patterned after a Masonic offshoot called The Mystic Order of Veiled Prophets of the Enchanted Realm (M.O.V.P.E.R.), formed in New York in 1889 for the purpose of "lively social relations, sometimes mischievous but never mean."

The Hijis (or Hyjis) did love to party and play practical jokes. They also seemed to like changing the name of their secret society whenever the mood suited.

Their annual event was a "Grand Ball Masque," at which members and guests were costumed as kings, queens and knights – even as "clowns and buffoons." If a newspaper clipping about one such event is to be believed, as many as 2,000 attended the 1893 masquerade

A GREAT ORGANIZATION.

A New Society That Has Jumped Into Popular Favor in Missoula.

Sunday at Odd Fellows' hall was perfected the organization of what is to be hereafter known as Monarch Moslem, No. 196, Sons of the Mystic Tie, an association of gentlemen banded for the diffusion of benevolence, charity and good will to all, its principal object being the elevation of man. At the meeting were present some twenty-five charter members, who selected from their members the following officers who are to serve for the ensuing six months:
Grand Hiji—C. E. Woodworth.
Vice Grand Hiji—F. W. McConnell.
Secretary—Chas. Searles.
Treasurer—A. W. Gould.
Veiled Prophet—Geo. T. Slack.
Medical Examiners—Drs. W. B. Parsons, H. H. Hansen.
Outside Sheik—Tylar B. Thompson.
Inside Sheik—J. J Dowling.
Grand Standard Bearer—C. A. Barnes.
Grand Marshal—J. T. Sawhill.
Master of Ceremonies—Wm. Jury.

Missoula Weekly Gazette, April 8, 1891.

The next dancing event will be the grand masque ball to be given March 8 by the Monarch Mosque No. 196, Sons of the Mystic Tie. This affair will have many of the features of a carnival. It will be held in the Missoula hotel which is now unoccupied. It is intended to make it entirely different from any masked ball ever held in the city.

Missoulian, February 28, 1893.

ball held at Missoula's Knights of Pythias hall. But count me as a non-believer.

The *Missoulian* newspaper, an apparent co-conspirator in the whole charade, described the event (just two years after the group was organized) as "the 82nd annual ball of the Moslem Mosque No. 196, Royal and Universal Order of Mystic Hijis." What happened to the Sons of the Mystic Tie?

The paper expounded, "Safe in the sense of disguise, hilarity was probably freer than witnessed at conventional socials, but the abandon was not of that character which even the prude would object to.

"One little plump and painted beauty, bubbling over with wit, flesh and good humor, clad in an expensive gown more plentiful in train than bodice, and with an attitude of toe that would be quite amazing even at a French ball, was pronounced the belle of the evening."

The reporter characterized another lady, a "handsome creature," as wearing "most of her costume on her head, her body enveloped in a filmy fold of gauzy texture, suggestive of a warm night and stifling atmosphere."

> Dresses decollette top and bottom, there were, and white lingerie, supplanted by dark and silken hose, left much to be imagined and little to be said. One handsome creature was noticed, most of her costume on her head, her body enveloped in a filmy fold of gauzy texture, suggestive of a warm night and stifling atmosphere.
>
> *Missoulian, April 13, 1893.*

But practical jokes and pranks most illustrated the character of Missoula's Hiji brotherhood.

One evening as midnight approached, "some hundred or more members of this mystic band" marched to the home of their "organizer," who had just consummated "his marriage to an estimable lady," and escorted the fellow to the Florence Hotel, "where the act of settin' 'em up at the expense of the groom was indulged in."

After considerable time, during which "soda water and other corks were kept flying in the air," the man thanked his fellow Hijis and appealed to them "to escort me hence to the spot whence I came."

On another occasion, the Hijis were reported to have appropriated the body of a murderer, who had just been hanged – placing his embalmed body upright in a downtown building. A note attached to the corpse proclaimed, "I am a Hiji and I am preparing for the Montana statue."

> **A WIERD TALE**
>
> **The Body of Burns Is Not In the Grave.**
>
> **A DIRE MIDNIGHT EXPERIENCE**
>
> Startling Discovery Made Last Night by a Missoulian's Alert Reporter.
>
> *Missoulian, December 31, 1892.*

The story, printed on the front page of *The Morning Missoulian*, was referenced a few days later in the *Populist* newspaper: "If what we have been told is to be believed, there is more truth than josh in that little story."

Keep in mind, the members of this "secret society" were prominent members of Missoula society, including George and Frank Higgins and Doctors Ellis and Hanson.

Perhaps the crowning achievement of the mischievous group was the elaborate theft of a Christmas turkey. But it also was the prank that led to the society's downfall.

Chapter 34

HIJINKS GONE BAD
THE GREAT TURKEY HEIST OF 1893

What follows is the account of a petty larceny – a story which would have been lost to history, but for the fact that the *Evening Missoulian* documented every aspect of the case – much of it on its front pages.

Why the newspaper did so is a mystery, but I strongly suspect that the paper's editor at the time, Lambert Molinelli, "a prominent member of the Knights of Pythias," not only knew every member of the group involved in the heist, but (perhaps) may have been part of their secret society, the Monarch Mosque No. 196, Sons of the Mystic Tie, or the Hijis, a brotherhood of highly placed pranksters and practical jokers.

TURKEY RACKET.

Cau·ing Heaps of Anxiety in Certain Circles.

PROMINENT MEN IMPLICATED

In the Swiping of the Toothsome Turk, for Which "Sheeney Kid" Now Languishes.

Missoulian, January 3, 1894.

Picking up their papers on the evening of January 2, 1894, Missoula residents read the following front-page account of what we'll call the Great Turkey Heist of 1893.

"Once upon a time there resided in Missoula, happy and fat, and totally oblivious to the dangers which surrounded him, a gentleman turkey of the dressed value of $2.

"Christmas came, as it does but once a year, and that turkey was selected to bring good cheer to the stomachs of some Missoulians. The turkey eventually fell to the lot of Charles H. Skinner, who resides at the Hammond block and who placed it on the window sill outside of his room that it might be kept fresh until the proper time should come to prepare it for the table, and there is where its job-lot of trouble commenced.

"On Christmas night, shortly after the electric lights had begun to throw their yellowish glare around the corner of Higgins Avenue and Front Street, that turkey disappeared: was 'swiped' in fact, and Mr. Skinner waxed exceeding wroth thereat."

So began the day-by-day coverage of the holiday bird's heist, which would carry on for the better part of a month.

A local bar-fly, Abe Cohen, known as the "Sheeney Kid," was promptly arrested for the theft, but "influential friends" rescued him from jail, promising Mr. Skinner they'd pay for the turkey and for his trouble.

The trouble is, they didn't pay up. So Skinner had the Kid arrested once again and brought before a city judge. Skinner told Judge Evans that those who offered to pay for his silence included two prominent Missoula doctors, Parsons and Hanson.

The Kid admitted that he and a man named George Earl had swiped the bird, but they did so at the behest of Parsons, Hanson and some others. The judge ordered the Sheeney Kid to be held in jail under $200 bond and issued a warrant for Earl.

Earl's trial was set for the following night and – given the press coverage – the courtroom was packed. "Every seat in the body of the house was taken, some holding portions of two and even three interested spectators, the gallery was crowded almost to suffocation, while even the press reserve on top of his honor's strong box was encroached upon by ordinary mortals."

The trial was a farce. Witnesses testified George Earl was involved, but the jury took only minutes to declare him "not guilty." Judge Evans, clearly exasperated, issued arrest warrants for Dr. W.B. Parsons, Dr. H.H. Hanson and Smith Davis for petty larceny.

Doc Parsons, indignant that his name be bandied about in "sidewalk twaddle," declared in a letter to the editor of the paper, "I had nothing to do with taking or eating the so-called goose (or paying for) hushing up the matter."

The Parsons-Hanson-Davis court appearance drew "the very cream of Missoula's male society," including "a number of gentlemen who have

> An investigation of the justice court records shows that Dr. Hanson and Smith Davis were arrested today for complicity in the turkey matter. Dr. Parsons has not been arrested, reports to the contrary notwithstanding, and this explanation is necessitated in order to dispel the impression prevailing that the latter named gentleman is also under arrest.
>
> There will be an extraordinary meeting of the Hijis held this evening, for the purpose of preparing bonds for the release of Smith Davis, a brother Hiji. All members in good standing are requested to be present as it is proposed to devote the proceeds from the last turkey banquet to this laudable purpose.

Notables arrested.
Missoulian.

John M. Evans, Courtesy Montama Memory Project, UM Acchives & Special Collections.

been directly and indirectly tangled up with" similar poultry pranks in the community, but have escaped "having their antics paraded in a police court in full view of a vulgar public."

As the two doctors stood before Judge Evans, Smith Davis hid "behind City Treasurer Curran's pen rack," a wise move given the fury of the judge, who immediately declared the two doctors in contempt of court and fined each $10.

> In passing sentence on these gentlemen, on the contempt proposition, Judge Evans characterized their conduct as reprehensible in the extreme, and said that while they might succeed, owing to the positions they occupy in society, in bull-dozing and black-mailing some people, that they had caught the wrong individual in him, and that such preposterous conduct in his court would not be tolerated for an instant.
>
> *Missoulian,*
> *January 4, 1894.*

As outlined indignantly by the judge, it seems "Drs. Parsons and Hanson had sworn out a complaint (with a local Justice of the Peace) ... charging Judge Evans with bribery (creating) a common rumor on the streets that a warrant had been issued" for Judge Evans' arrest in an attempt to "bulldoze" the turkey case. Evans declared "such preposterous conduct in his court would not be tolerated for an instant."

Still, the defendants won the day, convincing the judge that Dr. Parsons actually had nothing to do with the turkey stealing (his case was dropped) and, arguing they could not get a fair trial before Judge Evans, had the case transferred to Judge Donley's court.

It was late January when the case came before Judge Donley. The courtroom was packed, 30 witnesses were called, and County Attorney Denny "made a most eloquent appeal for justice (showing) plainly that the testimony unquestionably compromised the defendants." The defense simply asked that the case be dismissed, "alleging all sorts of things that had no bearing on the case," according to press accounts.

> **THE CONCLUSION**
>
> Of the Famous Turkey Swiping Contest.
>
> THE DEFENDANTS WHITEWASHED
>
> In Spite of the Conclusive Testimony Judge Donley Turns the Gentlemen Loose.
>
> *Missoulian,*
> *Janauary 22, 1894.*

Inexplicably, Judge Donley, "with his eyes averted from the gaze of every man in the room, almost inaudibly murmured that he could see no evidence to warrant a conviction and dismissed the defendants."

The prosecution was indignant. The *Missoulian* declared a "weak-kneed judiciary (had) succeeded in defeating the ends of justice" and the taxpayers were out a sum "sufficient to set the think pot of the average citizen working in a violent manner." In the end, only the lowly Abe Cohen, aka the Sheeney Kid, paid a price by serving jail time.

The case, while a monumental miscarriage of justice, was pivotal in the public shaming and slow demise of the Hijis.

They soon claimed to be indigent, failed to pay rent and were kicked out of the K of P Lodge. The *Anaconda Standard* newspaper reported, "The members of that mysterious order, the Hyjis, who were once proud of their organization, are today trying to disown membership."

The group garnered some press now and then in succeeding years, including an attempt to enter local politics with a "Hiji ticket" in 1900, but within a short time disappeared altogether.

MIGHTY HIJIS IN THE SOUP

Unable to Raise Funds to House the Goat They are Ruthlessly Hopped on By the Law.

The mighty have fallen. The noble order of Hijis has kerflunked. Monarch Mosque No. 196, Sons of the Mystic Tie, has been chucked, head over heels, into the consomme.

The recorder of Covenant lodge No. 6, I. O. O. F., yesterday afternoon instituted attachment proceedings against the Hiji organization, for $72, said to be due for rent of the lodge room in the Odd Fellows' building and Constable Tommy Corbett was started out on a still hunt for something to attach, that might, perchance, bear the trademark of the famous Hijis.

The fall of the Hijis.
Missoulian.

Chapter 35

LOU LOU, LO LO OR LOLO?

Lolo is a rapidly growing, three-stoplight community south of Missoula complete with a school awash in students, a renowned steakhouse and, in recent years, a popular brewery and distillery. Much of its population joins the daily Bitterroot Valley commute to jobs in Missoula.

Lolo is also chock full of history – Lewis and Clark, Travelers' Rest, Fort Fizzle, gold mining and Maggie Pickens.

When Maggie celebrated her birthday with a dance in the early 1890s, it caused quite a stir, at least with the resident contributor to a Missoula newspaper.

"They not only danced till the 'wee sma' hours, but until broad daylight," wrote the outraged community correspondent. "When parents uphold and themselves join in such wickedness ... when young girls know more obscenity than common sense ... then, why, in the name of humanity, do they send all the missionaries to foreign lands?"

That must have been some party!

Mining and the lure of riches brought many early white settlers to the area. In 1873, a group called the Buckly Company sank a shaft alongside Lolo Creek, finding gold "when down 13 feet and the quantity increased as they descended."

> Maggie Pickens celebrated her birth-day with a dance last Saturday evening. They not only danced till the "wee sma' hours," but until broad daylight. When parents uphold and themselves join in such wickedness; when girls, who should be playing with their dolls, must needs have beaux and lay aside girlish ways to ape womanly ones; when young girls know more obscenity than common sense; when girls of tender years are cared for by the police instead of their parents; when little boys find more pleasure in stealing than in attending school; when all these things 'occur in our own and immediate vicinity: Then why, in the name of humanity, do they send all the missionaries to foreign lands?
>
> *Missoulian, 1894.*

By the 1880s and 1890s, mining operations developed all around Lolo. One of the most notable was the "Chicaman" mine, described by a *Missoulian* scribbler as having tunnels of 250 to 300 feet and "a mountain of ore in sight, any of which may be worked as a profit."

The Chicaman produced thousands of dollars worth of gold, although records of production have been lost to history. Other mines included the Champion, Dixie, Forlorn Hope, Red Bear and Mollie C.

But little known to most of today's residents is the fact that Lolo wasn't always called Lolo. Early on, it was called Lou Lou, Lo Lo or Loo Loo. No one seemed to agree, including map makers and local newspaper reporters.

In 1883, the *Weekly Missoulian* lobbied for a wagon road to be built to "Lou Lou" hot springs.

> Wm. Strange returned from a two weeks stay at Lou Lou Springs, Tuesday, much improved in health.
>
> *The Western News, Stevensville.*

The *New Northwest* newspaper in Deer Lodge, in its coverage of the non-treaty Nez Perce movement out of Idaho into the Bitterroot Valley in 1877, referred to the "Lo Lo" trail.

As far as the United States government was concerned, the matter should have been settled in January 1888.

According to a newspaper clipping, "A petition for a post office at Lou Lou ... has been sent to Washington, and it is expected that the office will be established in a few days. John F. Delancy will be the postmaster and they will spell the name the old way 'Lo Lo.'"

But an 1896 timetable for the Bitter Root branch railroad still listed the stop as "Lou Lou." As late as 1914, that spelling was still being used in a newspaper account of a funeral: "The Lou Lou Lodge of I.O.O.F. conducted the burial ritual of the order."

> N. P. TIME TABLE.
> BITTER ROOT BRANCH.
>
> | SOUTHBOUND | | | NORTHBOUND |
> |---|---|---|---|
> | No. 213, Pass. | | | No. 214, Pass. |
> | 7:40 p m Dep. | Missoula | Arr. | 7:10 a m |
> | 7:49 | Bitter Root | | 7:01 |
> | 8:04 | Lou Lou | | 6:39 |
> | 8:26 | Florence | | 6:13 |
> | 8:45 | Stevensville | | 5:50 |
> | 9:06 | Victor | | 5:30 |
>
> *Ravalli Republican, May 27, 1896.*

Officials of the Lolo National Forest believe its namesake probably evolved from "Lou Lou," a pronunciation of 'Lawrence,' a French-Canadian fur trapper killed by a grizzly bear and buried at Grave Creek."

Maybe.

Some of the most exhaustive research into the name was done by Joseph Mussulman and others who created the "Discovering Lewis and Clark" website in the 1990s. Mussulman, who passed away a few years ago, described the research as "a careful and thorough inquiry into the history of Lolo as a place name."

Early railroad map, 1897. Courtesy Montana Historical Society Research Center.

Mussulman could find no reference to "Lolo" in the Lewis and Clark journals, but discovered that David Thompson, an early trapper and trader, mentioned the name "Lolo" for the first time in 1810 – a reference to a fellow traveler.

But it wasn't until the 1850s that a variation of the name "Lo-Lo" appeared as a place name on a map, so was there a connection?

The map was designed by Washington Territory Governor Isaac Stevens. He had hired John Mullan to explore possible railroad routes over the mountains. Mullan's guide, Gabriel Prudhomme, is believed to have told Mullan that the creek and nearby trail used by Lewis and Clark was known by locals as the "Lo-Lo Fork" or "Lo-Lo's Fork."

But when Stevens drew a map of the area, he labeled the creek "Lou Lou Fork." Some folks think it was just a typesetter's error.

Here's another story: John Owen, who established Fort Owen in Stevensville in 1850, often noted a person named Lolo in his letters and business ledgers. This may have been an Indian who worked for one of Owen's clerks – and that leads to a curious tale.

Mussulman wrote: "Jackson (the clerk) returned to his lodge at the close of day to discover that rascal Lolo was ... very comfortably stowed away in the bed with Mrs. Jackson. She confessed that the two of them had made plans to steal some horses and elope. Mr. Jackson resigned the next morning and hit the road with his wife. Whether Lolo hung around or took off too was not recorded."

Could the Indian named Lolo be the namesake of the creek and town? Perhaps.

When he died, his remains were said to have been buried at "Graves Creek" near Lolo. There's a notation on an old map, marking the spot.

Lolo National Forest Supervisor Ralph Space, using that old map, found the site and a headstone in 1939, but by the 1960s the area was logged and the site was destroyed.

Finally, in 2003, a cadaver dog was used, the "presumed remains" were found and a historic marker was erected at the spot.

So what was the actual etymology of the town's name? Was it "Lawrence (Lou Lou)," the fur trapper killed by a bear? Was it the Indian named "Lolo?"

Something to ponder as you have a steak dinner or a local brew at the businesses bearing that name in the small community just south of Missoula.

Chapter 36

WHAT'S IN A NAME?
THE CRACKER CITY AND THE BABY COUNTY

We humans like to name things, quite often for what they look like or sound like. Naming things, of course, is useful for finding your way about.

Natives referred to this region as the "Country of the Mountains" or "Shining Mountains."

Joaquin Miller, who published his book *"Illustrated History of Montana"* in 1894, proposed calling the region's inhabitants, "Montanese." He much preferred that to "Montanians." Neither took.

Not satisfied with names alone, we also seem enamored with "nicknames." In Leeson's *"History of Montana, 1739-1885,"* Montana nicknames included "The Magic City" for Billings, "The Queen of the Mountains" for Helena, "The Beautiful City" for Bozeman, "The Silver City" for Butte and "The West Butte City" for Missoula.

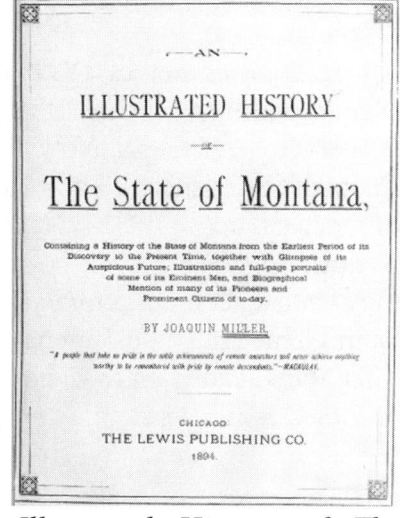

Illustrated History of The State of Montana, by Joaquin Miller, 1894.

The trouble with nicknames is they aren't always terms of endearment – they can, in fact, ridicule. Such was the case with a couple of nicknames in the late 1800s. Missoulians derisively referred to one of their neighbors as the "Baby County" and referred to Helena as the "Cracker City."

The "Baby County" was a short-lived reference (chiefly by the *Missoulian* newspaper) to Ravalli County after it split from Missoula County in 1893. "Poor little Ravalli County," wrote the paper, "the baby county of Montana, torn asunder from old Missoula County ..."

Poor little Ravalli county; poor tax-payers of little Ravalli county. Since its creation, the baby county of Montana, torn asunder from old Missoula county, has had a legal experience in criminal matters that bids exceeding fair to bring its rate of taxation up to and considerably beyond the highest notch reached anywhere within the confines of the state for several years past.

Missoulian, April 21, 1894.

More than 100 years later, little Ravalli County is still around – poor, perhaps – but increasingly popular for its lifestyle and cost of living, borne out each day by the thousands of Bitterroot commuters headed to jobs in Missoula.

As for the "Cracker City," if you look up the etymology of the word cracker, you'll find it was a derogatory term for poor white people in the rural South in the 1800s. It also referred to the crack of whip or a loud braggart. Hmmm, loud braggarts? Helena? Politicians? Perhaps.

It turns out the nickname began as a complimentary reference to Helena's economic growth, which was then turned sideways by opposing forces during the final campaign to choose a capital city for Montana.

In the summer of 1891, representatives of the American Biscuit Manufacturing Company (that's right – a cracker company) visited the "Cataract City."Geez! Now I have to explain another moniker. "The Cataract City" is Great Falls – so named, not as a reference to the malady of the eyes, but to the city's namesake cascade of waterfalls.

Anyway, the biscuit boys told a local *Tribune* newspaper reporter they hadn't yet made a final decision where to locate their cracker plant. Both Great Falls and Helena had the cheap water power they needed. Then they headed on to "The Queen of the Mountains" for a visit.

In October 1891, they announced their choice – Helena would be the site.

> *A CRACKER FACTORY.*
>
> Among the great enterprises projected by the energetic, wide-awake citizens of Helena is a $50,000 cracker factory. That city is bound to create a pay-roll. It has looked over the field with an eye to that end and finally decided on a cracker factory. A year or
>
> *Great Falls Tribune,*
> *June 6, 1891.*

The *Great Falls Tribune* immediately mocked the enterprise, pointing to Helena's long history of failed economic schemes. "There is one thing about Helena … she always aims high if she does shoot low," adding, "She should have it. It will add at least three men to her present payroll."

The next year, "Helena for Capital" badges appeared, bearing the image of a gingersnap (from the cracker factory) trimmed out with a ribbon. The *Livingston Enterprise* called it "a novel idea, but not so handsome in design as several of the badges distributed by other contestants."

The *Anaconda Standard*, tongue in cheek, suggested maybe they should add a small cracker to their Anaconda copper button. The *Helena Independent* newspaper responded: "The suggestion is good. The Helena cracker factory will be running day and night when the Anaconda copper works have passed into a reminiscence." It didn't quite work out that way.

Over the next few years, the *Missoulian* newspaper (which strongly backed Helena for the state capital) routinely used the "Cracker City" reference in news stories large and small.

"Dr. Parsons took this morning's train on a short business visit to the Cracker City." "Herr Daniel Bandmann and wife returned last evening from the Cracker City, where they gave a very successful performance of 'Rip Van Winkle.'"

A few months before the 1894 election, which pitted Anaconda against Helena for Montana's capital, there was a brief labor dispute at the cracker factory, a golden opportunity for the *Anaconda Standard*.

In its story titled "The Climax," the newspaper wrote: "It is useless to deny that a fearful crash has come; that a totally unexpected crisis has been reached; that the industrial world has experienced a shock which tends to destroy the nature and relation of things that involve them all in hopeless confusion, chaos and collapse ... far be it from this newspaper to seek to magnify any evil, or appearance of evil ... let us all be calm and brave."

> Far be it from this newspaper to seek to magnify any evil, or appearance of evil, particularly at a period like this of sad misgivings, universal uneasiness and suppressed excitement.
>
> *Anaconda Standard,*
> *April 15, 1894.*

Right. After a number of lengthy paragraphs, we're told "an amicable settlement has been reached and the strike declared off."

Short term, Helena won the capital designation. Long term, the Anaconda Company far outlasted the biscuit factory. And the moniker "Cracker City" soon enough faded from use.

Of course, our penchant for naming and renaming continues. The "Magic City" of Billings is now referred to by many as "B-Town." "Eastern" is now "MSU-B." Many in Bozeman now refer to their city as "The Bozone." It seems we just can't help ourselves.

Chapter 37

TODAY'S WEATHER
FLIES, ANTS & FORECASTER FAWCETT

If the house flies are buzzing about madly or if fleas are numerous, expect wet weather or hail. On the other hand, if gnats are swarming in the sunshine, you're sure to have fair weather.

And, don't even get me started about ants; they're responsible for every which kind of weather.

I know – these days everyone just checks their smart phones or tunes in to the radio or TV for the forecast, but it was a bit different back in the 1800s. Many people relied on folklore or local weather sages.

> A flock of geese passed over town Sunday night going north, and the weather prognosticators say it is a sign that winter has not come to stay.

Big Hole Breezes, Wisdom, October 27, 1899.

A man named Tice from Radersburg visited Helena in June, 1880, telling a reporter from the *Weekly Herald* "that the weather will remain cool until the 22nd, when warm, summer weather will set in." Mr. Tice's information was "generally proven correct," according to the *Herald*.

Henry G. Vennor, calling himself a "practical meteorologist," sent out letters to Montana newspapers prophesying that late December, 1883 and early January, 1884 would be unusually mild – "even summer weather."

Not so, declared John X. Biedler.

The Fort Benton River Press quoted Biedler "prognosticat(ing) a three or four day storm at the time of the next new moon, on the 29th (of December). X. says he can double discount Vennor in Montana as a weather prophet."

A number of weather gurus built national reputations including "Professor Blake of Kansas" and "Reverend Ira R. Hicks, the Missouri weather prophet." Their prognostications were carried in papers

John X. Beidler, member of the Montana Vigilance Committee and Collector of Customs in the 1860's, UM Archives, 1880.

across the country.

Critics, though, accused them of profiting from the ignorance of the people. One wrote, "As long as the common people are kept from knowing how to read a United States weather map," he wrote, "so long will Hicks remain a superhuman being in the eyes of the uneducated."

Scientific weather forecasting began in the mid-1800s. The telegraph made it possible to gather volunteer weather reports from enough locations, in real time, to predict the direction and speed of large storms.

In 1870 the Army "Signal Service," was created "to provide for taking meteorological observations...and for giving notice...by magnetic telegraph and marine signals, of the approach and force of storms."

Signal Service Fact Room, circa 1881, Library of Congress.

At first, forecasts were given for large regions. By 1886 forecasts narrowed to "states, or parts of states." Locally, the Signal Service used everything imaginable to communicate their forecasts to the public, from flags and balls to steam whistles and bells. Eventually they settled on a series of white, blue and black flags to announce weather changes.

It would have been great to know what it was like to be an early day Signal Service employee, but no one documented their lives. Luckily in

1922 Henry Williams, a Weather Bureau employee, realized the pioneers of the Signal Service were getting old, and their stories would be lost to history. So he asked many of them to write down their recollections.

But the papers were never published and did become lost for a time – hidden away at the National Archives – until uncovered in the 1990s.

One old-timer recalled the Signal Service as a tough life – after all, they were in the Army.

They endured everything from bed bugs at training camp ("They kept us scratching for a living throughout the summer of 1881.") to long shifts on the job ("I was expected to take the 6:36 a.m. observation and stay on until after the 10:36 p.m. observation was taken and filed.")

An Army regulation read, "Unnecessary conversations, writing of private letters, and reading of newspapers during office hours are strictly prohibited. Conversation necessary to the proper dispatch of business will be carried on in a low tone of voice."

In April 1876, one graduate of the Signal Service School of Instruction at Fort Myer, Va., nearly froze to death hiking to the Mountain Meteorological Station on Pikes Peak and the Base Station at Colorado Springs.

In 1885 Signal Service "rookies" undergoing their initial training at Ft. Myer endured such severe verbal abuse they complained to the top brass, but it backfired. The whole class was court-martialed. Finally, Congress investigated and decided to convert the whole meteorological division to a civilian operation.

At times, local townsfolk were a bit wary of this new "science" and particularly its associated equipment.

J. W. Smith of the early Signal Service wrote, "My predecessor at a small southwestern station at Corsicana, Texas, told me that soon after establishing his station he was waited on by a committee, appointed by dissatisfied citizens on account of the very unsatisfactory weather conditions caused by the meteorological instruments as there had been no such weather before 'them things were set on the roof.'

"All the explanations that could be made proving unsatisfactory, the official suggested

Professor Cleveland Abbe, meteorologist and assistant to the Chief Signal Officer, 1912, Library of Congress.

they adjourn to the cafe over the way for further discussion, where it cost our man about $25 for sufficient refreshments to convince the committee that the weather instruments were not at fault."

In Missoula, early-day weather reporting fell to William ("W. B.") Fawcett. Known as "a man of considerable refinement," Fawcett had attended Irish colleges and, in his youth, had traveled much of the continent – even serving in various European armies. As a non-commissioned officer in France, he fought in a border war with Germany.

When he came to America and eventually to Missoula, he was hired as a surveyor for the Northern Pacific railroad. Later he set up an assaying business.

He was fascinated by the weather, serving as the local "displayman" for the Signal Service, erecting a weather service flagpole to fly the variety of six-foot-square colored flags (white cloth for fair weather, etc.).

Fawcett ran unsuccessfully for a few political offices including County Surveyor and Justice of the Peace in Hell Gate township. He died alone in a "bachelor home" at 221 East Cedar Street (now Broadway) under mysterious circumstances on December 10, 1900 – a morphine bottle found in his room.

Frank Leslie illustration, May 1, 1880, courtesy NOAA's National Weather Service (NWS) Collection.

Weather Prognosticator Fawcett is in receipt of the series of government flags which are to be displayed, as conditions warrant, from the observatory staff now being erected at the Lucy block where the station is to be located.

Missoulian, May 1, 1894.

As scientific weather forecasting become more commonplace

in the late 1800s, public interest in and respect for the service and its forecasters grew. "In some places (the forecaster) was as important as the postmaster."

"It was during the great storm of '88; all wires were down, there was a dearth for news and the ambitious 8 page paper of a western town had to be filled. Frantically the editor dispatched two of his men to the weather office.

"The next morning...the entire front page was devoted to weather; weather of past years, weather on Mount Washington, weather forecasting, weather here and hereafter."

Today, over 100 years later, weather is still often given the lede in the nightly TV newscast and weather personalities still tend to be popular; the big draw for local TV news ratings.

They never seem to mention the ants though.

Chapter 38

THE WORKING GIRL
THE CURIOUS CASE OF THE CROCHETED TIDY

The setting: Missoula in the late 1800s, Justice Court, Judge Ross presiding.

The defendant: Frank Jurden, accused of cat-burgling a tidy (a small receptacle for one's odds and ends), valued at $5.

The victim and complainant: M'lle Leontine David, who discovered the theft upon returning home from her ... ah ... shall we say ... nighttime endeavors.

OK, fine. She was a working girl, a lady of the night, but a victim nonetheless.

> **LAWYERS GALORE.**
> An Exciting Trial Held in a Justice Court.
>
> *Missoulian, June 20, 1894.*

The local paper described her as "a poor orphan girl, who through unfortunate circumstances, had been thrown upon this cold and clammy world and compelled to eke out her own existence and who could, therefore, ill afford to lose the article in question or any other article possessing a monetary value."

The county attorney had multiple witnesses and felt he had a "lead-pipe cinch" of a case.

The defendant, a foul-mouthed miscreant known widely in the community, seemed to have no case at all. Who would even defend him in court?

> The defendant had been arrested and ruthlessly thrown into a felon's cell on Saturday evening last, charged with having appropriated a crocheted tidy valued at $5, belonging to a poor orphan girl who, through unfortunate circumstances, had been thrown upon this cold and clammy world and compelled to eke out her own existence and who could, therefore, ill afford to lose the article in question or any other article possessing a monetary value.
>
> *Missoulian, June 20, 1894.*

Well, it turns out, the answer to that question was: most all of the legal luminaries of Missoula!

When the seemingly minor $5 theft case was called, Jurden was surrounded by "a formidable array of legal talent, consisting of Messrs. Marshall & Corbett, Messrs. Bickford, Stiff & Hershey," along with a half-dozen other top lawyers of the city.

The legal lights sat quietly as the victim's neighbor and good friend, Miss Georgie Allen, told the jury she saw the defendant with the stolen tidy and confronted him. She said Jurden responded to her accusation with a barrage of epithets that "caused her great pain and subsequent loss of sleep."

> Wing Chung Lung, a prosperous Chinese merchant and manager of the slickest opium joint in all Hell Gate township, swore that he saw this "belly man" hop out of Miss Leontine's boudoir window with something bulky concealed under his coat.
>
> *Missoulian, June 20, 1894.*

Testifying next, reported the *Missoulian*, was "Wing Chung Lung, a prosperous Chinese merchant and manager of the slickest opium joint in all Hell Gate township, (who) swore that he saw this 'belly man' hop out of Miss Leontine's boudoir window with something bulky concealed under his coat."

The most reputable of the prosecution's witnesses was local weather prognosticator W.B. Fawcett, who claimed he was in the vicinity of Miss David's place (solely "in his official capacity" as a weather observer) when he saw the defendant's "peculiar conduct."

> W. B. Fawcett, the next witness, testified that he was in the neighborhood of Miss David's residence, on Saturday evening, in his official capacity as weather prognosticator, in and for the city of Missoula, and that he noticed the prisoner and his peculiar conduct. Questioning the man regarding his actions he was rebuffed by the latter, who threatened to perforate his hide with an assortment of leaden pellets, and followed up the threat by accusing him of things that were absolutely unbecoming his station in life.
>
> *Missoulian, June 20, 1894.*

When he confronted Jurden, Fawcett claimed the defendant "threatened to perforate his hide with an assortment of leaden pellets" and accused Fawcett of "things that were absolutely unbecoming his station in life."

The cadre of defense lawyers, the finest in the Garden City, surprisingly "made no attempt to refute the testimony of the prosecution."

In its closing argument, the prosecution told the jury the evidence was self-evident; after all, the defense didn't dispute any of the accounts or allegations.

The hour was drawing late when the defense had its turn at closing arguments. First they asked the judge if they could "argue the case in shifts, so that all could have an opportunity to repair to their respective homes for dinner," but the request was denied.

> it. The legal gentlemen did not make any attempt to deny the theft of the tidy but insisted that the prosecution had not proved that it was a crocheted tidy as alleged in the complaint and demanded an acquittal as the result of this very important omission. The jury grasped the idea at once and did their part by bringing in a verdict of "not guilty." The gladdened prisoner fell upon the necks of his overjoyed counsel and promised to reimburse them all handsomely on the 11th, 12th, 13th and 14th days of July.
>
> *Missoulian, June 20, 1894.*

So they commenced their "general, all-around denial" that the defendant had anything to do with the theft. Then the elite legal defense team played its ace.

The prosecution, they proclaimed, had failed to prove the pilfered container was a "crocheted" tidy (as charged) and "demanded an acquittal as the result of this very important omission."

The jury "grasped the idea at once" and, on that technicality, found Jurden not guilty.

Late 19th century justice, Missoula style.

But the question remains – why would a dozen of Missoula's most respected attorneys come to this man's defense?

The *Missoulian* newspaper explained it this way.

Jurden, a "sort of assistant horse trainer" at the Missoula racetrack, had "summoned the entire legal fraternity of the city ... by various promises of 'straight tips' and other inside information" concerning the July horse races.

The paper concluded: Upon hearing the jury's verdict, "the gladdened prisoner fell upon the necks of his overjoyed counsel and promised to reimburse them all handsomely (with tips on the horse races) on the 11th, 12th, 13th and 14th days of July."

There was no follow-up report, I'm sorry to say, on how those tips paid off. But it can be reported that one week after the trial, Jurden was hauled before Judge Ross on a charge of disturbing the peace, pleaded guilty and was sentenced to 60 days in jail.

Chapter 39

POLSON'S COWBOY BAND
CLARINETS, TROMBONES & SIX SHOOTERS

It was called Polson Market Day – the first one held Saturday, April 30, 1910. If successful, the town would stage one each month.

Everyone was invited to bring items they wanted to sell and an auctioneer would put them on the block – horses, pigs, cows, buggies, household goods – anything. Merchants did the same.

> **Look Everybody!**
>
> On Saturday, April 30, 1910, and On Every First Saturday in Each Month Thereafter, Polson, Mont., will hold a big
>
> **MARKET DAY**
>
> There Will be Sold at Public Auction, Horses, Wagons, Saddles, Cows, Pigs, Buggies, Harness, Machinery Household Goods, Etc., Etc.
>
> Bring whatever you have to sell. Your goods will be auctioned off free of charge.
>
> Every merchant will sell goods on that day at a particularly low price and many prizes will be given.
>
> Some amusement will be furnished, either a band, a ball game or a big Kootenai war dance. Come everybody, see the fun and profit by the big bargains.
>
> *The Flathead Courier, April 21, 1910.*

The Carey Blacksmith Shop offered to "give a 10 percent discount on all grain beds." Shur Brothers said they'd "shoe four of your horse's feet at the cost of three." And, Flathead County State Bank promised to "give each depositor, large and small, a fine Morocco leather check book holder."

A week before the inaugural event, the town's newly minted local paper, the *Flathead Courier*, suggested "some amusement will be furnished, either a band, a ball game or a big Kootenai war dance." They weren't sure what.

It turned out to be a group of twelve musicians, each a professional player at some point in his life in "some of the best bands in the country," coming together to form the "Polson Band."

The newspaper was ecstatic, reporting there would be four singers backed by clarinets, cornets, a trombone and a couple of drums – and, each of the musicians "owns his own instrument"!

The paper urged locals to turn out and give the new band their "cordial support." After all, said the paper, "(A) town without a band is like a ship without a rudder."

The crowd loved them. They not only played for the event, but "also serenaded the principal places of business," in the evening.

In a matter of months the band had become the main attraction at local events. On the 4th of July they performed a concert at the waterfront, then led a parade from the docks to the fairgrounds. As many as five thousand people turned out.

In the coming years the group, now 30 strong and renamed the "Polson Cowboy Band," would play at events all over the region, promoting the city by the lake, declaring "Polson Does Things!"

Cowboy Band in Missoula, circa 1914.

At the Missoula Stampede, the band proved so popular they were held over for the entire event. After daytime performances, they would hop into a number of cars and roam about Missoula – "making themselves heard."

The Garden City newspapers, according to the *Courier*, had given the band great reviews, winning "a home in the hearts of stampede crowds and (making) a lasting impression of the Power City's enterprise."

The singers and musicians were even hosted at a luncheon sponsored by the Missoula Mercantile company.

Later, Professor Marion Riffo, the band's director, told Missoula news reporters they would not only be back to perform at the Stampede again, but they would be bringing the entire town!

The boisterous Riffo said, "We're coming down by the hundreds and you'll know it when we arrive." A fifty-car caravan was being organized. So many Polson residents plan to come to the Stampede, he continued, that "those who don't come will feel pretty lonesome."

By the time of the next summer event, the Cowboy Band was boasting there would be "nearly 100 automobiles" for their "impressive entry at the northern end of the city," with "six shooters, horns, bells, megaphones...a pet mule and a grizzly pup."

When the band arrived, one press account said the city was "at once plunged into the merry making which was continued...until late at night."

Missoulian, July 3, 1920.

Falthead Courier, May 11, 1922.

In the next few years though financial support for the band diminished and the group folded. In 1922 the Flathead Courier reported, "A few practices were held this winter but with no money with which to purchase new music and no backing the interest lagged.

But the Polson Cowboy Band did eventually reinvent itself performing at local events including the Polson Harvest Festival. It peaked again in the mid 1930s.

In 1934, a "Junior Cowboy Band" was formed and in 1935, as part of the $15,000 Polson dock and breakwater project, the *Missoulian* reported "a pavilion will be built for the accommodation of the Polson Cowboy Band and their outdoor band concerts."

After that, press reports about the band (except for numerous "look back" stories about its heydays in the early 1900s) stopped – nothing to be found.

But, what a group it must have been.

Chapter 40

A FOWL AFFAIR
MISSOULA'S GREAT POULTRY SHOW

More and more folks these days seem to be turning backyards into barnyards, installing chicken coops and posting photos of their feathered family members on social media.

I'm awakened most mornings not by an alarm clock, but by my neighbor's rooster.

By the way, if you want to hear some fabulous fowl flourishes, check out soundbible.com. They even have one audio file titled "Pissed Off Duck."

Such are the melodies resonating through many neighborhoods nowadays as local governments approve chickens, ducks, quail and more to the list of approved backyard fowl.

Historically, these refrains have been routine in Montana, and proudly so.

In 1914, Missoula hosted the Montana State Poultry Show at the old Gem Theater building on West Front Street, downtown.

The business community backed the exhibition, big time. Carpenters were busy for more than a week, creating display rooms. Missoula Light & Water Company provided all the electrical and lighting work needed, and Sid Coffee, the neighborly druggist, "donated the disinfectant dope which will be used unsparingly so that both fowl and human will be safe.

OLD GEM THEATER FULL OF PRIZE CHICKENS.

STATE POULTRY SHOW OPENS THIS MORNING WITH GREATEST LOT OF BIRDS ON RECORD.

Missoulian, January 27, 1914.

"Every train that pulled into Missoula seemed to be a chicken special," chirped the *Missoulian* newspaper. "Every express car unloaded crate after crate of birds, and the trucks that moved up to the platform were piled high with coops, resembling, in size, loads of hay." There were entries from all across Montana, as well as Idaho and Washington.

By the time the poultry pageant opened, there were well over a thousand feathered favorites roosting in the showrooms.

Judge George Holden of Owatanna, Minnesota, upon first seeing the displays, told reporters the show would likely outclass any such exhibition "held between the Twin Cities and Spokane."

SHOW IS TOO LARGE FOR JUDGE HOLDEN
State Poultry Exhibition Opens and Crowd Throngs Room All Day—Greenfield Comes to Help Score Birds—Record Score Made by Helena Bird—Room Too Small.

Missoulian, January 28, 1914.

At the same time, he declared he couldn't possibly judge so many birds by himself, and an emergency call went out for another judge to be rushed in from Butte to help out.

More than 500 people attended the poultry party on the first afternoon and, by evening, organizers gave up trying to keep count.

Similarly, it was hard to count the birds. There were White Leghorns, White Plymouth Rocks, Barred Rocks, Silver Campines, Single Comb White Orpingtons, White Wyandottes, Rose Comb Rhode Island Reds and most every other variety, as well as some ducks, geese and turkeys. Joe Wells, a "well-known colored man of this city who claims to be 107-years-old" and who was an accepted expert in the field, called it "the finest show I ever saw under one roof."

Henry Tripp, "breeder of the famous Blue Jacket strain of Barred Plymouth Rocks, and Dr. Asa Willard, owner of the Bitter Root flock of the same breed of birds, cleaned up most of the prizes in that class," reported the local paper.

MISSOULA FANCIERS WIN A BIG VICTORY
Tripp, Willard, Bisbee Brothers and Other Local Breeders Carry Off Honors in Some Big Classes at Poultry Show—Interest Increasing in State Exhibition.

But the "high honors," the "sweepstakes," went to D. L. Doig of Sixteen Mile for a "good old Brown Leghorn." Doig also picked up the Chicago, Milwaukee & St. Paul Railway Cup, valued at $50, for the best-scoring pen of partly colored birds.

Then, as now, a lot of folks didn't realize some of their friends were "chicken fanciers" until they noticed the names on the coops.

The 1914 *Missoulian* pointed out: "There are a large number of these well-known people (who are chicken fanciers) at the show this year and it is one of the encouraging signs of the times in the chicken world. From an interest taken in a pen of birds kept in a small coop in the backyard – perhaps a corner of the woodshed – has often been developed a strong liking for poultry and a big yard of choice birds."

Of course, that sort of expansion is unlikely today, given municipal limitations on the number of chickens, ducks and other fowl allowed in residential areas.

For those concerned over the sweet "essence of bird" wafting across your neighbor's hedge, show the true Montana spirit spirit and plant some fragrant western junipers, jasmine, peonies or a Star Gazer lily to freshen the atmosphere.

Or if you're a bit devilish and wish to respond in kind to your kindly neighbor, you could plant a Starfish Cactus. I'm told its flowers put off "a rather horrifying odor."

Then there's always the Voodoo Lily or the Corpse Flower. Just remember: The wind blows both ways.

Chapter 41

BASEBALL FEVER IN MISSOULA
Potatoes, Rutabagas And Onions Fly Through The Air

Missoula has always had a rocky romance with baseball. In a recent spat, many fans booed the name change for Missoula's boys of summer from Osprey to PaddleHeads. The new mascot is a moose, and the team colors are shades of hunter green.

But remember, a couple decades ago when Play Ball Missoula leaders stood in a vacant riverside lot, pitching the idea of professional baseball returning to Missoula, that too was controversial. And so it's been, back through the eras of the Timberjacks and the Highlanders, even as far back as the 1800s when it seemed everyone in town had baseball fever.

Baseball field south of Clark Fork River, Missoula, circa 1899. Courtesy UM Archives & Special Collections.

One 19th century newspaper columnist reported, "Almost any object that has the slightest claim to spherical shape is pressed into service in the absence of a regulation baseball; old and tired potatoes, last year's rutabagas, Herculean onions and many other similar objects may, at times, be seen flying through the air and chased by some one of the many ball fiends."

In the 1890s, the Missoula nine played their games at Union Park on East Main Street, and while they would engage just about any team willing to ride the rails to Missoula, many (if not most) of their games were against "post" teams from Fort Missoula.

The sportswriters of the day were brilliant but, unfortunately, must go without credit since bylines weren't yet the fashion.

Fort Missoula baseball team, 1902, photo by Morton John Elrod. Courtesy UM Archives & Special Collections.

Here's a description of an umpire (a soldier by the name of Crupper), whose "calls" were ... well ... questionable: "This individual appeared on the field resplendent in a white linen suit, having for a background a lavender shirt, cut very much on the decollete order, a cute little black and white striped traveling hat adorning his very dark head. As an acrobat and jumping jack, the gentleman is simply 'out of sight,' but as an umpire he is a trifle the worst that has ever been perpetrated on suffering humanity. Mr. Crupper has umpired his last game in the city of Missoula."

One early and comic fundraiser drew a crowd of 200 and the following press clipping: "Two misfit nines, one professing to represent the enterprising little town of Bonner and one equally nervy in respect to the Garden City, inflicted their audience yesterday afternoon with a game of alleged baseball that was remarkable only for its rankness.

"The new diamond at the ballpark was covered with dust, sand and pebbles to a depth of six inches, which fact coupled with a job lot of miserable batting, an aggregation of errors that would be inexcusable even in a 'kid' game, and an exhibition of all around head-achey playing caused the little band of spectators to regret even the charitable purpose which had brought about its presence."

Loyola High School baseball team, 1913, on their ball field. Courtesy UM Archives & Special Collections.

Over the years, fan interest and financial support has ebbed and flowed. In 1914, the directors of the Missoula franchise were forced to "regretfully recommend the berth occupied by the Missoula baseball club in the Union Association be relinquished." By contrast, the same year, the Garden City's Indoor Baseball League was flourishing. The opening game featured the pennant winners from the league's first two seasons, the Marathons and the Athletics. The Federals and the University rounded out the four-team league.

Whether known as the Federals, the Marathons, the Timberjacks or now, the PaddleHeads, Missoula seemingly will always have a baseball team, and the fever that accompanies it.

Chapter 42

DIETING ADVICE
WALK IN SNOW, MOVE TO DENVER, OR COMMIT A FELONY

Happy New Year! Time to make those resolutions.

The top pledges in recent years, according to folks who poll such things, have been "to be a better person," followed closely by "losing weight" and "exercising," the two perennial favorites.

Despite the odds, I'm opting for the two perennials. For advice on how to accomplish my goals, I'm turning to the pages of Montana newspapers past.

First I need to access my current state of corpulence.

Dr. Benjamin Ward Richardson, an eminent British physician, in one of his widely circulated articles from *The Asclepiad*, re-published by newspapers across America including the *Great Falls Leader*, in November of 1888, poses a pivotal question: As you awaken from a night's repose, do you "still feel oppressed by a sense of weariness?" Do you have a desire, "almost irresistible, to go to sleep again?"

Ah, well – yes, I do.

A-hah, exclaims Dr. Richardson, it appears you have a severe case of languor, caused by an accumulation of a "diffusible and light chemical substance, which acts after the manner of an intoxicant...to the nervous system."

Benjamin Ward Richardson.

The cure, he says, is simple: "exercise and the wearing of clothing which will give free liberation to the exhalations of the skin." Get outside, says the good doctor, in "the most perfect purifier" known – "atmospheric air," and be sure to wear what we, today, call "moisture-wicking clothing." An article in the *Helena Independent* in 1890 offers further, more specific advice on the

Great Falls Leader, November 7, 1888.

nature of my outdoor exercise. It should involve running barefooted in "freshly fallen snow." Five minutes, at first – then, a half hour at a time.

A REMARKABLE PANACEA.

The Free Cure of Father Kneipp, of Voerishofen, the Latest Fashionable Fad.

Walking Barefoot in Wet Grass, Cold Water or Fresh Snow.

A Cold Bath Without Drying, a Farinaceous Diet, Moderate Eating Among the Many Means Employed.

The Helena Independent, December 22, 1890.

Now after my refreshing barefoot run in the snow, I am instructed not to dry my feet but "to put on dry socks (and boots)...and, then take a smart walk."

The article asserts such exercise has "entirely cured a woman of chilblains and a girl of toothache," adding, "These are only typical cases among numerous cases."

Wow. I can lose weight and avoid the dentist with one simple barefoot daily run in the snow.

Alternatives include bowling, "the most invigorating of all amusements" (1870), dancing, which "brings in play all the muscles" (1898), or curling, "one of the most healthful exercises imaginable (1899)."

But, the 1883 *Rocky Mountain Husbandman* newspaper points that exercise alone is not the answer. My eating habits must change as well. The daily amount of food and work must be in balance "like the accounts of an honest bookkeeper."

Letter on corpulence, 1865.

But, which diet to choose?

In the 1860s William Banting abandoned exercise (it simply led to a more "prodigious appetite") and began researching all sorts of diets.

In 1865, declaring he had found the answer, he published a pamphlet on "Corpulency & Leanness" recommending fresh fish, dry toast, and considerable claret, sherry or Madeira. Lots of alcohol – that's appealing.

For the purists, there was the "French Water Diet." Alas, an article in the 1886 *Butte Semi-Weekly Miner* debunked the theory, quoting a Dr. DeBove as saying "the quantity of water taken has no influence on body weight."

The *Anaconda Standard* had a story recommending we avoid certain "tabooed articles." By doing so, one might lose "15 pounds within six weeks." Feel free to eat meats of all kinds, but avoid "sweets and starches," says the 1897 article. Wait a minute – that sounds like today's Atkins Diet.

More research reveals there are lifestyles that require neither diet nor exercise to achieve weight loss.

The simplest and easiest of weight-loss plans involves moving; not moving in the sense of physical exercise, but moving...to Denver.

A story in the 1880 *Helena Herald* declared if a 200-pound man were to move from the East to mile-high Denver, in two or three months he would become "a 175-pounder." Even more weight could be lost by moving to Leadville, Colorado, (elevation two miles above sea level) but, you'd have to leave your pet behind. "Very few dogs, except hounds, can live in Leadville, and no cats survive there."

Helena Weekly Herald, Great West, Denver, Colorado. November 4, 1880.

Another simple lifestyle change is described in the *Billings Herald*. It carried a story from the *Atlanta Constitution*, quoting a prison official as saying, "leanness and meanness seem to go hand in hand." There was not, he said, a single Georgia prisoner over 200 pounds.

But, committing a felony, particularly in Georgia, seems a bit extreme in my search for svelteness.

And, that same prison official made a persuasive argument to ditch this whole dieting thing and pursue the good life. "A fat man," he said, "is always contented." He eats well, sleeps well and laughs a lot. "A man who can do (that) does no murder, theft, robbery and bears not false witness against his neighbor."

Lean & Mean, Atlanta Constitution.

One could carry that philosophy even further, as did the Stevensville newspaper, the *Western News*, in 1907. Quoting dietary experts, the paper recommended, "Eating before going to bed, particularly if one is up late (as) being most favorable to thorough body repair that the blood at night be rich in nourishment."

Maybe I have it all wrong. The 1898 *Anaconda Standard* says this whole New Year's resolution thing is a slippery slope. Their editorial staff concludes it unwise "to take a pet fault and resolve against it."

They recommend something small – something achievable. "If we put our nineteenth-century vigor to work we may kill the habit before the twentieth dawns.

"The good resolution day is upon us. Do not less it pass unheeded, and do not abuse it. Let us all resolve some one thing and carry it to a successful finish no matter how small it may be."

DANGERS OF DIETING

UNDERFEEDING LIABLE TO WEAKEN HEART'S ACTION.

Usually Appetite Is a Measure of Health, and the First Sign of Illness In a Man or an Animal Is Loss of the Desire For Food.

The Western News, Stevensville, February 6, 1907.

I think I'll change my resolution to "being a better person," while eating, drinking and making merry. Happy New Year!

Chapter 43

SNAKE OIL
RESTORE MANHOOD, CLEAN YOUR LIVE & STAVE OFF INSANITY

It's called "Direct to Customer" (DTC) advertising and it's pervasive in today's media. Big pharmaceutical companies use it in TV ads, urging you to "ask your doctor if (this or that drug or pill) is right for you," following which they list the sometimes lengthy side-effects of the drug.

According to AdWeek, a major publication that monitors trends in advertising, pharmaceutical companies in recent years have spent nearly $5 billion annually on drug advertising, although there have been attempts in Washington, D. C., to reign that in.

In a way, DTC is nothing new.

Back in the 1800s, before any federal oversight, all sorts of products were being marketed directly to customers via the media of the day – the daily and weekly newspapers – with claims to cure everything that ailed you.

They became known as patent medicines or, in less kindly terminology, "snake oil remedies." They were advertised regularly in Montana newspapers; some were available at local drug stores and others by mail.

Cupidene claimed to cure back pain, insomnia, pimples and even "unfitness to marry... all the horrors of impotency." Said to be the "prescription of a famous

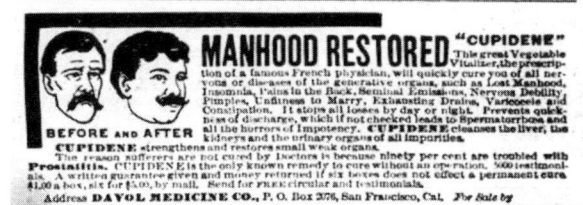

Cupidene ad.

French physician," the Devol Medicine Company of San Francisco claimed Cupidene would restore your manhood, and clean your liver and kidneys at the same time.

Decades later, postal authorities would issue a fraud order against the company when the federal Department of Agriculture determined the ingredients were nothing more than ash and sugar combined with "starch, red pepper, Spanish flies and fibrous tissue."

Another pitch, for Aphroditine, guaranteed to cure "any disorder of the generative organs... (including) seminal weakness, hysteria, nocturnal emissions, loss of power and impotency, which if neglected often lead to premature old age and insanity."

If you had a drinking problem, "You had better stop at once or you'll lose your job," and, of course, the best way to stop drinking was by taking "Orrine," available at the Missoula Drug Co. at Higgins and Front.

By 1921, Dr. Arthur J. Cramp, the Director of the Propaganda Department (I am not making this up) of the American Medical Association published the "Nostrums and Quakery" book, declaring that Orrine was mostly just milk sugar and ammonium chloride.

Aphrodotine ad.

If you had "bronchitis, croup, stiff neck, asthma, neuralgia, congestion, pleurisy, rheumatism, lumbago, pains and aches of the back or joint, sprains, sore muscles, bruises, chilblains, frosted feet, or colds of the chest," then you needed Musterole. Yes, Musterole would do it all. It even claimed to prevent pneumonia.

Ladies with unsightly hair were first admonished for their carelessness, then urged to buy Newbro's herpicide. "Many ladies are, and many more should be, ashamed when they look in the glass and see their hair. The condition of some is almost a disgrace. Thin, scraggy, wispy hair generally indicates dandruff, which is due to a germ."

Nostrums and Quackery book, by Dr. Arthur J. Cramp, 1921.

Musterole ad.

Once Montana's ladies had taken care of their unsightly hair and were fit to be seen in public, they presumably rushed to stores like the D. C. Smith Agency in Missoula for Stearns' Pile Remedy, for it promised to stop the pile pain "in one minute," or your money back.

Of course, if your back ached or you were having bladder trouble, you were told to stop eating meat immediately and take four ounces of Jad Salts from your local pharmacy. After all, "Nearly all rheumatism, headaches, liver trouble, nervousness, dizziness, sleeplessness and urinary disorders come from sluggish kidneys." So you should "take a tablespoon in a glass of water before breakfast and in a few days your kidneys will act fine."

In 1905, *Collier's* magazine ran an article by Samuel Hopkins Adams titled, "The Great American Fraud," in which he exposed these snake oil marketers.

Stearms' pile ad.

"Gullible America will spend this year some seventy-five millions of dollars in the purchase of patent medicines. In consideration of this sum it will swallow huge quantities of alcohol, an appalling amount of opiates and narcotics, a wide assortment of varied drugs ranging from powerful and dangerous heart depressants to insidious liver stimulants; and far in excess of all other ingredients, undiluted fraud. For fraud, exploited by the skilfulest [sic] of advertising bunco men, is the basis of the trade.

"Should the newspapers, the magazines, and the medical journals refuse their pages to this class of advertisements, the patent medicine business in five years would be as scandalously historic as the South Sea Bubble, and the nation would be the richer not only in lives and money, but in drunkards and drug-fiends saved."

Aside from patent medicines, there were other 19th century suggestions for improved health.

How about bowling? That's right, Ben Lindsay's Bowling Gymnasium

Bowling gymnasium ad.

at the St. Louis Hotel in Missoula offered "Cures guaranteed without the use of medicines, by practicing at the most invigorating of all amusements, bowling."

Then, in the early 20th century, there was something called "open air schools," an experiment conducted in conjunction with the Society for the Prevention of Tuberculosis.

> OPEN-AIR SCHOOLS SUCCESSFUL

Open air schools ad.

Detailed in Polson's *Flathead Currier*, in 1910 (from an article in the *American City Magazine*) the concept was to expose school children to more sun and air, both summer and winter.

In Providence and Boston, as well as in European cities, the open-air experimenters had removed one wall of a school house, allowing in fresh air (extremely cold air in winter) in order to "harden children to weather conditions."

The author of the article was Eleanora Whitman Curtis, "holder of the degree of Master of arts and honorary fellow of Clark University."

Curtis concluded, given that "delicate and backward children can accomplish in far less, sometimes in half, the time the task of ordinary schoolchildren, raises the question as to whether similar methods in elementary school instruction might not be adopted to the benefit of all school children. On the grounds of social hygiene alone, then, outdoor schools would seem justifiable. On the pedagogical side they are a revelation."

Chapter 44

BICYCLE TRIP TO THE BITTER ROOT
"GOD BLESS THE MAN THAT DISCOVERED BEER"

Bicycling is a big deal in Missoula.

The city boasts, "With over 22 miles of off-street trails and 40 miles of on-street bike lanes, Missoula is a great place to ride...(and) the League of American Bicyclists has designated the city a Gold level Bicycle Friendly Community."

There are certainly outspoken fiscal detractors, but with the addition of the South Reserve street overpass and the completion of the Bitterroot trail, one can now bike all the way from Missoula to Hamilton in style.

It wasn't nearly that easy during Missoula's first bicycle boom, back in the 1890s. Not only were there no bike trails back then, there were few roads!

U. S. Army, 25th Infantry Bicycle Corps. James A. Moss commanding, 1897, Courtesy UM Archives & Special Collections.

Fort Missoula was famous, of course, for its U. S. Army Bicycle Corps, but bicycling was was extremely popular with local citizens, as well.

What follows is an eye-opening account of an attempted Missoula-to-Hamilton bike ride over 120 years ago.

Here it is, verbatim, from the *Anaconda Standard* newspaper, published June 25, 1895:

Missoula, June 24th – One of the most eventful pilgrimages ever taken from Missoula by Missoula people was the bicycle tour taken yesterday by Messrs. Chaney, Taylor, Griffin, Howard and Hathaway.

The party left here early in the morning and from the time they rolled over the bridge until 10 last night, when they straggled back into town, two of them in a buggy, the trip was one continued round of accidents, mishaps and casualties.

The Lonely Wheelman, circa 1890s. Courtesy UM Archives & Special Collections.

If the party had started out to see how much trouble it could have, it would have been impossible to have scared up anymore, unless the day could have been lengthened several hours.

When Canby Morrison this morning cleaned out the buggy in which he brought in two disabled bicycles and their dilapidated riders he found a notebook in which one of the riders had kept a log of the trip.

This he gave to a *(Anaconda) Standard* reporter this morning and it is reproduced here, to show how much grief can be crowded into one day.

It is not known which of the wheelmen wrote the record, but it is none the less interesting for being anonymous:

Sunday, June 23rd, 4 a.m. - Just got up. All on hand but Chaney. He did not go to bed 'till two and doesn't want to get up. Weather clear and fine.

4:30 – Chaney up. Breakfast cooking. Have overhauled the wheels and everything is ready for the trip to Hamilton.

5:00 – Breakfast eaten. We are off in a bunch. Chaney, Griffin, Taylor and Howard all in good form.

5:03 - Crossed the bridge all right. All felt so fine that we speeded up crossing the flat. Went too fast for the start. At the Congregational Church Cheney fell all over himself, dented his machine and bruised his knee.

5:05 – Fresh start made. Chaney rather groggy. Using language not be coming to a gentleman, especially on Sunday morning. Howard had a narrow escape from a header.

5:30 – Crossed the Bitterroot railroad. Chaney feeling better. Wheels all running well except Chaney's, whose machine was wrenched in his fall at the church. Had no business to pass a church on Sunday morning, anyway.

6:05 – Crossed the Buckhouse Bridge. Road very dusty. Good breeze to keep us cool. Took a drink. Not much good. Too heating.

6:50 – Over the Lou Lou grade. Pretty stiff pedaling. Griffin's wheel acting badly. Slips a cog once in awhile.

7:25 – Had a good run across the Lou Lou Flat. Road still dusty. Took another drink. Miles are getting pretty low. Man that paced them must have had long legs.

Taking a rest, circa 1890s. UM Archives & Special Collections.

7:55 – Passed Carlton. Bitter Rooters don't know what to make of us. People climb on fences to see us go by. Not much dust here. Griffin's wheel suffering from lost motion.

8:20 – Best run we had from Carlton toward Florence. Griffin's wheel has all gone to pieces. Pedal loose. Stopped for repairs. Took a drink.

8:30 – Tom Hathaway overtook us while Griffin's wheel was being repaired. He is having a good trip. Says he'll go with us to set the pace. We are off again.

9:55 – Roads rough. This Sunday wheeling isn't what it is recommended to be. Taylor and Howard running easily. Decided to take no more drinks. Whiskey is to heating. Had to walk about two miles.

10:15 – Wonder who is road supervisor here. He's no good. Terrible roads and too many irrigating ditches. Stevensville in sight. Griffin's wheel working like a barrel churn, steady by jerks. Wish we hadn't thrown away that bottle.

10:30 – Crossed Stevensville bridge. Chaney's knee is lame. Griffin's wheel is lame, too. Weather getting pretty hot.

11:10 Stevensville looks mighty fine. Think we'll stop here and make permanent repairs to Griffin's wheel. Will take lunch here. Beer is a better drink for hot weather than whiskey.

12:20 – Lunch tasted good. Wheel repaired and now we're off for Hamilton.

12:45 – The man who named this district Aetna was all right. It's hotter than any well-regulated volcano ought to be. The dust is six inches deep. We can't see each other, it's so thick. Beer is unquestionably better than any other beverage.

1:15 – Walking. Dust too deep for riding. Tom Hathaway says that this is fun. Nobody else thinks so. Our faces are streaked with dust and perspiration. Missoula is a good place to spend Sunday.

1:25 – Still walking when we are not standing still. Fearful dust storm blowing. Wish we'd stayed at home.

2:30 – Have been able to ride some distance. Road still dusty. We can see Corvallis, but don't think that we will get there. Not much fun pumping through this dust. God bless the man that discovered beer.

3:00 – Homeward bound. Hamilton is too far away. Unfortunately Missoula is still farther. Dust, dust, dust.

4:00 – Out of the dust belt once more. Eyes, ears, nose, mouth, all full of fine, gritty particles. Beer all gone.

4:35 – Stevensville in the sight again. More beer there. Irrigating ditches have played havoc with our wheels.

5:10 – Had rest at Stevensville. Have a package of egg sandwiches and five bottles of beer. Thirty miles to Missoula.

5:15 – Beginning to rain. This soil may be all right for agricultural purposes, but when it's wet it isn't good road material.

5:25 – Shower over. Dust flies up in chunks as our wheels go through it. These irrigating ditches are rough on wheels.

5:40 – Chaney's rear tire is getting loose. He says he didn't put shellac enough on it. Somebody ought to buy him a barrel of it.

5:55 – That tire is getting looser. It has worked the valve loose and we will have to go into dry dock to fix it.

6:15 – Have fixed the valve and had some beer. Chaney chewed some gum and stuck it around the leak. Then tore off a strip of cloth from his clothing and bandaged it.

6:30 – Stopped for lunch. Feel better now. Been raining here and roads muddy. Off for home.

Identified only as "Carl H. on a bicycle" – circa 1890s. Photo by William Arthur Hoblitzell. Courtesy UM Archives & Special Collections.

6:45 – Progressing slowly. Tom Hathaway fresh as a daisy. All the rest getting jaded except Howard. Wish we had a team.

7:30 – Tried to get George Dalglish to take us home, but he had no room in his rig.

7:45 – Cheney's wheel is getting worse. Griffin's is bad, too. All the rest are all right. It's mighty hard pumping. Beer all gone.

8:10 - Overtook Dalglish again, but he had no room. Canby Morrison and Charlie Dorman in sight. They have only one horse, though.

8:30 – Cheney's wheel has slumped. Griffin's is not much better.

Morrison has loaded the two wheels on behind and has taken the two wheelmen aboard.

8:45 – Hathaway, Taylor and Howard still pumping along. Mud deep and sticky. Wheels catch about 50 pounds of it on the tires. Chaney and Griffin keeping pretty quiet.

9:00 - Mud so deep that wheelmen have to walk. Canby's horse giving out. Mighty hard sledding.

9:10 – Lyon and Williams passed us in a rig. Offered us friendly counsels and advice.

9:25 – Passed another man with busted wheel – Francis. Gave him Griffin's, which was not so badly disabled as his. Took his wheel on the buggy.

9:30 – Missoula in site. Horse can't hold his head up. Don't know whether we'll have to walk or not.

9:50 – The horse held out. Chaney and Griffin are home at the hotel.

10:05 – Taylor, Hathaway and Howard reached home. They rode all the way. We will not go next Sunday.

Chapter 45

THE GARDEN CITY – DOES MISSOULA EVER GIGGLE?

She has been described as having an "air of neatness and comfort." Others deemed her a "horrible place," of "unblushing wickedness."

One person summed up the place as "a nice pretty little city, but (with) no thrill," prompting the question: does Missoula ever giggle?

What a variety of opinions about Montana's Garden City!

The *Montana Post* (Virginia City), in late 1866, described Missoula as "a sprightly little village containing about twenty houses."

The writer, under the pen-name, "Everywhere," went on to say, "The first cabin was built here in December 1864, and shortly after a saw-mill was erected. Messrs. Worden and Higgins have just completed a large flouring mill, thirty six feet square and three stories high...(at a) cost over thirty thousand dollars."

Montana Post, Virginia City, 1866.

Four years later, Missoula's first newspaper, *The Missoula and Cedar Creek Pioneer,* described the area as having "the most fertile bottom lands (where) five hundred bushels of potatoes to the acre is not an uncommon yield (and where) watermelons, tomatoes, cucumbers, and the important root crops flourish luxuriantly."

Thus, the name: Garden City.

The *Pioneer* also noted the area was "dotted with the homes of well-to-do farmers (with) the air of neatness and comfort (offering) convincing proof of the existence of thrifty settlers."

The editor of the *Madisonian* newspaper was quite taken by Missoula after a visit in 1877. Thomas Deyarmon said, "A great many people who have never visited....have an impression that it is a village with only a country store, post office, blacksmith shop, and tavern...

"Visitors to Missoula for the first time express surprise at the elegant stores and private residences which adorn the place."

Missoula County as viewed by Madisonian newspaper, 1877.

In 1883, the *Walla Walla Statesman* noted, "What Seattle is to the lower country, Missoula is to the mountains (with) the same energetic class of people who are determined in spite of everything."

That was a reference to the "old-timers;" men like C. P. Higgins, Frank Worden and W. J. McCormick, not the "soft youths fresh out of the states" who "continually deride" such men.

"With unparalleled liberality," said the *Statesman*, the old-timers offered the Northern Pacific company just about anything they wanted to bring the railroad to Missoula. "These men have been here waiting almost against hope for 25 years for the (NP) to penetrate the mountains and change the wilderness into a garden."

But the city's growth, spurred by the railroad, brought problems, too.

—We are told that one of our clerical residents recently made the remark that he had in his life viewed many of the lowest dens of infamy in New York and Philadelphia; but that the streets of Missoula after nightfall were hell compared to anything he had ever seen. Strangers who have come within our gates have also dropped some very uncomplimentary remarks regarding the unblushing wickedness of our town,

Missoula is wicked as hell, Missoulian, June 1, 1883.

The *Missoulian* newspaper noted that strangers to town had been dropping "some very uncomplimentary remarks regarding the unblemishing wickedness of our town." Even a local resident had remarked "the streets of Missoula after nightfall were hell compared to anything he had ever seen" - even the "lowest dens of infamy in New York and Philadelphia."

Warts and all, Missoula was still a beautiful place.

In the summer of 1887, The *Cincinnati Illustrated News* sent a couple of photographers out for two weeks to capture "a series of views of the town" to be included in a write up of the city.

MISSOULA TO BE ILLUSTRATED

Professors Park and Frank, represents the photographers of the Cincinnati Illustrated News, are engaged in making a series of views of the town. They also write up the city. This will be a grand advertisement for Missoula, and will be of great benefit for friends in the east. These gentlemen are first class artists and are highly spoken of by press and public. Their stay will be limited to two weeks.

Missoulian, July 29, 1887.

A year later, in 1888, *Northwest Magazine* published an extensive piece about Missoula, including some compliments of the local newspaper's newly-completed building.

The paper, it said, "occupies a part of the finest building in Montana owned exclusively by a newspaper publisher. In external appearance it is the handsomest building in Missoula county."

My favorite description of Missoula-past comes not from newspaper editors, but from a coed at Montana State University (now, U-M).

In the spring of 1917, "students in Freshman English classes at the university were asked to state their judgments of Missoula."

The local paper picked one essay, that of Miss Este Shannon, for publication, calling it "clever and discerning." Here it is.

"Missoula is, to me, just like a schoolteacher I used to have in the fifth grade. Her name is Miss Adams. She is an ordinary, pretty, young American of a middle-class family, but perhaps a little more quiet and reserved.

"She looks more like a small-town music teacher than a grade school teacher. Her clothes are of good material, of conservative style, and she always wore a suit two seasons. Her brown hair was always very smooth. Everything about her was 'nice.'

> **Missoula Nice, but Too Sedate, Student Thinks**
>
> Can you imagine Missoula giggling? Miss Este Shannon, a freshman at the State University, is sure Missoula never relaxes her characteristic primness long enough to giggle. Students in Freshman English classes at the university were asked recently to state their judgments of Missoula. Miss Shannon's theme is clever and discerning enough to deserve publication. It follows:
>
> *Missoulian, March 12, 1917.*

"On Saturday she helped her mother cleanup, on Sunday she went to church and then took a walk in the afternoon, and on Mondays she got up early to help with the family washing.

"Missoula is such a nice pretty little city, but it has no thrill, no colorfulness, no sparkle. It's a good convenient place in which to acquire book-knowledge, or to grow old.

"But even when Missoula is being frivolous – even Missoula has carnivals and circuses – she looks a little stiff and strange. She has the air of looking on at the fun, rather than participating in it.

"Just like Miss Adams, at the church dances, who always looked pretty in her best clothes, but spoiled it all by her self consciousness and embarrassment.

"Missoula smiles quietly and rather sweetly at you any sunshiny day, but can you imagine our Missoula giggling?

"Missoula is rather precise. Her streets are named after trees, men and their families, in the most matter-of-fact way you ever saw.

"If only it was more vivid, it would be charming."

Chapter 46

A KANGAROO IN ST. REGIS

It's a dilemma, a predicament, a quandary. The problem is, I can't swear to the veracity of the story to follow.

On the one hand, it's plausible – given what little I know about the St. Regis area. On the other hand, it does sound a bit far-fetched. Just a bit.

You be the judge. This is the tale – unedited in any way by me – straight from a Missoula newspaper on February 28, 1894.

A PECULIAR DISEASE.

Experience of a Missoulian Back-Wood's Correspondent.

Missoulian, March 7, 1894.

"It is not often that your correspondent attempts anything in the line of journalism, and it is not among the impossibilities that the *Missoulian* and its host of admirers will be just as thankful if, after this effort, I should retire to my lonely hut in the back woods and never again attempt to make myself heard in this direction.

"There is not, as might be expected, any news of a general nature transpiring in this out-of-the-way place worthy of mention.

"At this season of the year, we have nothing but snow and ice and lots of them, but I, personally, had an unusual experience a night or so ago that has worried me not a little and, owing to its exceeding peculiarities, I believe that it might prove interesting enough to *Missoulian* readers.

"On Friday night, tired and worn out through overindulgence in dancing affairs and the banquets which are so numerous in this mountain retreat, I quenched my thirst with a couple of glasses of sparkling St. Regis water, blew out the gas and crawled into my downy couch.

after midnight I was awakened by a cold breath on my burning cheek, and sitting up beheld, to my horror, a huge kangaroo hopping around the room. The animal must have measured, when standing erect, fully eleven feet in height. His tail as it wound around the little room, could not have been less than nineteen or twenty feet

Missoulian, March 7, 1894.

"Shortly after midnight I was awakened by a cold breath on my burning cheek, and setting up beheld, to my horror, a huge kangaroo hopping around the room.

"The animal must have measured, when standing erect, fully 11 feet in height. His tail as it wound around the little room, could not have been less than 19 or 20 feet long; his ears, sticking up like a government mule's, were certainly not less than 2 feet in their extreme length; and the sharp, glistening toenails, for which these animals are famous, were in this instance fully 9 inches in length and seem to me to possess the strength of a woodman's axe.

"All of this I hastily surveyed while conjuring in my mind some means of winning the battle that I knew was bound to occur with my decidedly unwelcome visitor.

"I have a fine collection of guns and other weapons hanging on a rack directly over my couch and I reached up and took down the first rifle my hands came in contact with. It happened, however, to be an old three-barreled muzzleloader that had been made to order for Kit Carson, and not been loaded for over 70 years.

"The kangaroo took in the situation at a glance and sat down on his haunches in the middle of the room and gave vent to a series of short, grating laughs so peculiar to the animal in his native clime.

> I have a fine collection of guns and other weapons hanging on a rack directly over my couch and I reached up and took down the first rifle my hands came in contact with. It happened, however, to be an old, three-barreled, muzzle loader, that had been made to order for "Kit" Carson, and had not been loaded for over seventy years. The kangaroo took in the situation at a glance and sat down on his haunches
>
> *Missoulian, March 7, 1894.*

"He or she, however, evidently concluded to take no chances, as guns that are never loaded are always the most dangerous, and, doubling itself up as much as possible, made a leap for the window.

"The animal's tail, in switching around to get in line with its body, made a half hitch around my right leg and I was quickly dragged to the window.

"I caught hold of the lower sill and hung on for dear life, the animal pulling one way and your unfortunate correspondent the other.

"The night was a cold one, and by a superhuman effort, I managed to hold on against the superior strength of the animal, until its tail froze solid and broke off, when the animal bounded away into the darkness of the night, and I fell back on the floor, limp and faint.

"This tale, or tail, may seem hardly worthy of belief, but I still preserve about 6 feet of the kangaroo's rear appendage which I shall bring with me on my next visit to Missoula, and will probably present it to Bob Foster, as I believe it will make a most acceptable addition to his already famous cabinet of curiosities.

"In narrating my decidedly novel experience, I have been roundly laughed at and frequently been called upon to account for the presence of such an animal in this section of the country.

"I was unable to do this for a time, but am informed by no less a personage than a prominent railway official who visited St. Regis yesterday, that a monster kangaroo, in fact the largest of his species in existence, had escaped from the circus which was wintering in California and when last seen was rapidly making tracks in a northwesterly direction, and I do not entertain the slightest doubt that my visitor of Friday night was the same animal, who favored me with an impromptu call on his way to the North Pole.

> I desire to state, by the way, that I had not been to Superior or Saltese, for several days prior to this incident, neither had I been drinking anything stronger than St. Regis water, which I am informed is chemically pure, nor had I been, during the previous week, perusing any of Violette Gleamer's Saturday gush and salaciousness. KANGAROO JOE.

Missoulian, March 7, 1894.

"I desire to state, by the way, that I had not been to Superior or Saltese for several days prior to this incident, neither had I been drinking anything stronger than St. Regis water, which I am informed is chemically pure, nor had I been, during the previous week, perusing any of Violet Gleamer's Saturday gush and salaciousness. – Kangaroo Joe."

So there you have it – unabridged, unedited, just as it appeared in 1894.

Surely, you'll agree with me that such a story, albeit unsubstantiated, is absolutely plausible, therefore likely absolutely true.

After all, it was in the paper. I rest my case.